THE AIR FORCE IN SOUTHEAST ASIA

THE B-57G -- TROPIC MOON III
1967-1972

by
Richard A. Pfau
and
William H. Greenhalgh, Jr.

OFFICE OF AIR FORCE HISTORY

Headquarters USAF, 1978

Published by Books Express Publishing
Copyright © Books Express, 2012
ISBN 978-1-78039-651-4

Books Express publications are available from all good retail and online booksellers. For publishing proposals and direct ordering please contact us at: info@books-express.com

FOREWORD

(U) As in World War II and the Korea police action, the enemy in Southeast Asia sought the protective concealment of darkness to move his troops and supplies. Although U.S. tactical aircrews cut roads and destroyed moving vehicles during daylight hours, they were ineffective at night. Jungle vegetation and mountainous terrain amplified their difficulties in finding and attacking the trucks, watercraft, and troops that poured southward each night through the maze of roads, footpaths, and streams that constituted the so-called Ho Chi Minh Trail in eastern Laos. Casting about for an aircraft capable of interdicting the infiltration flow at night, the Air Force finally settled on a modified B-57 as the most suitable vehicle on which to mount and test new sensors and weapons in a night attack role.

(U) Conceived in 1967 as Project Tropic Moon III, the B-57G was the first jet bomber specifically configured for self-contained night attack sorties in Southeast Asia. Within a relatively short time, the Air Force modified, tested, and flew the B-57G against hostile targets. When the Air Force decided that the time had come to withdraw the B-57Gs from Southeast Asia, Secretary of the Air Force Robert C. Seamans, Jr., wrote to the Chief of Staff of the Air Force that "it seems to me appropriate that we record and evaluate our experiences with the B-57Gs from concept formulation through redeployment to highlight those lessons which would be valuable in developing and employing similar systems in the future." That task was assigned to the Director of

Operations in the office of the Deputy Chief of Staff for Plans and Operations at HQ USAF. Maj. Gen. Clifford W. Hargrove, the Deputy Director of Operations, asked the Chief of Air Force History for "assistance in preparing a historical study of the B-57G program . . . . "

(U) Mr. Richard A. Pfau a temporary staff member of the office of the Chief of Air Force History, undertook the task of preparing the desired monograph. Although he found most of his material in the files of the Albert F. Simpson Historical Research Center at Maxwell Air Force Base, he exploited other repositories wherever possible. Before he returned to his university studies, Mr. Pfau prepared a first draft of the desired study. That manuscript and his notes remained inactive until early 1977, when they were sent to the Albert F. Simpson Historical Research Center for historical review. Mr. William H. Greenhalgh, Jr., a staff histrian at the center, conducted additional research, edited Mr. Pfau's work, and added material where necessary. The result is this study of the B-57G program from inception to termination.

CONTENTS

	Page
FOREWORD	iii

Chapter

		Page
I	NIGHT ATTACK AIRCRAFT SYSTEMS	1
	Background	1
	Advocates of Night Interdiction	5
	Operation Shed Light	6
II	TROPIC MOON III	12
	Concept and Definition	12
	The Statement of Work	16
	Funding Problems	19
III	THE B-57G	23
	The B-57B	23
	Eighteen Months of Delays	25
	Testing, Training, and Problems	31
	Deployment Preparations	38
IV	IMPROVEMENT EFFORTS	41
	Forward Looking Radar	41
	Pave Gat	45
	Video Recorder	50
	Long-Range Navigation (LORAN)	52
	Other Improvement Efforts	53
V	COMBAT OPERATIONS	55
	The 13th Bombardment Squadron, Tactical	55
	The Deployment	61
	Commando Hunt V	64
	Equipment Problems	73
	The Rainy Season	79
	Commando Hunt VII	85
VI	TERMINATION OF TROPIC MOON III AND SUMMARY	90
	Return to the United States	90
	The Air National Guard	91
	Summary	93

	Page
NOTES	95
ABSTRACT	111
ACRONYMS AND ABBREVIATIONS	113
APPENDIX I	117
APPENDIX II	125

ILLUSTRATIONS

MAPS

B-57G Deployment Route	62
Steel Tiger Reconnaissance Sectors	65
Steel Tiger East	68
Road Network, Central Laos	80

CHARTS

B-57G Equipment Layout	17
Mean Time Between Equipment Failure	36
B-57G Configuration	55
B-57G Contract Progress	59

PHOTOGRAPHS

B-57G (four views)	34
B-57G Modified with Pave Gat System	46
B-57G with Two External Mk-84 Laser Guided Bombs and Four M-36E2s in Internal Bomb Bay	71
B-57 External Carriage of Mk-82 Laser Guided Bomb (500 lb)	71
M-36 Incendiary Bomb	71

CHAPTER I -- NIGHT ATTACK AIRCRAFT SYSTEMS

Background

(U) Military forces traditionally have felt more secure when hidden by the blackness of night while shifting forces, moving supplies, building defensive works, or otherwise preparing to attack enemy forces or withstand an assault. Even though possessing certain disadvantages, night movement has been used widely throughout recorded history as part of military operations. With the advent of the military aircraft, night movement became even more essential, particularly in the earlier years before night flying was practical. Observers in balloons and observation aircraft during World War I directed accurate artillery fire and an occasional air strike on enemy troops and vehicles during the daylight hours, forcing both sides to confine most of their troop and supply movements to the hours of darkness.

(U) Between the end of World War I and the outbreak of World War II, most air forces placed little emphasis on night aerial reconnaissance or night tactical air strikes. Tactical aviation became highly effective during the early months of World War II, forcing both sides to limit their surface movement to the night hours once more. Each side then sought aircraft that could prevent night movement. The British Beaufighter, although used primarily as a night interceptor aircraft, also performed well as a night intruder to harass enemy night movement. The United States tried the P-70 and the P-61 Black Widow in that role, with little success, and conventional bombers such as the B-17 and B-25 unsuccessfully attempted night missions against motor transport and other logistic targets. Nevertheless, some form of night interdiction was essential to military success. When the Germans below Rome were cut off from northern Italy by effective day interdiction, for example, they continued to supply their forces, and even to shift divisions, by moving only at night.1/

(U) Similarly, the Japanese forces in the Pacific made good use of darkness to carry out movements largely denied them during the day by U.S. Army and Navy aircraft. The Army successfully used a few B-24 bombers, reconfigured for night snooper operations and redesignated SB-24s, against shipping and well-defined island targets, although the inflated claims of their crews cast some doubt on their true effectiveness. Experiments with P-38s and other single-place aircraft demonstrated the inability of a pilot alone to cope with the myriad actions required on a night intruder mission. To illuminate their targets, some squadrons tried dropping flares, which not only proved undependable, but also were more of a hindrance than a help since they alerted enemy defenses, thus increasing the threat to the strike aircraft. The variety of weapons, illuminants, procedures, and aircraft tested in the Pacific failed to improve the night tactical interdiction capability.2/

(U) At the start of the Korean war, the Air Force again did not have a single unit trained for night intruder operations or an aircraft suitable for such a mission. The F-82, an escort fighter modified for night intercept operations, proved a failure, even though it did shoot down the first enemy aircraft of the war--in daylight. Its successor, the jet-powered F-94, was almost as unsuccessful, unsuited for either night strike or night intruder missions. Okinawa-based B-29s flew many night bombing missions against the growing North Korean fighter opposition, but their targets were fixed and rather easily located. The entire night intruder mission became the responsibility of the B-26, an obsolete World War II light attack bomber formerly designated the A-26.3/ Once again the fighting ended without any significant improvement in the ability of the U.S. Air Force to stop enemy movement at night.

(S) Well before the fighting ended in Korean, combat flared in Southeast Asia. The insurgent communists (the Viet Minh) already had learned to conceal their movements from their opponents--the French military forces--by moving only at night or during bad weather. Once the Viet Minh defeated the French and launched their campaign against South Vietnam and Laos, they achieved maximum speed and efficiency by moving largely by day because their opponents lacked airpower. As South Vietnamese aircraft became more numerous and U.S. aircraft appeared on the scene in the mid-1960s, the North Vietnamese moved more than 80 percent of their vehicles at night. Because both the South Vietnamese and U.S. aircraft were ill-equipped for low altitude night operations in the mountainous terrain of Southeast Asia, the North Vietnamese succeeded in maintaining the flow of troops and supplies to South Vietnam, even though darkness slowed their convoys. Early in 1964 the U.S. Air Force and Navy concentrated their attacks against targets in North Vietnam, greatly reducing the number of night attacks against infiltration targets in Laos. U.S. Navy air crews used A6A aircraft with moving indicator radar features to locate vehicles and deliver ordnance, but with less than satisfactory results.

Typical of these results: when ground observers reported 154 enemy trucks along a particular stretch of road, Air Force air crews were unable to find a single vehicle. During one period when 514 night sorties covered the road system of eastern Laos, the pilots claimed the destruction of only eight trucks. In desperation, the Air Force even used F-102 interceptor aircraft with infrared sensors to find targets and to attack them with rockets. The short range of the sensors and the poor performance of the aircraft at low altitudes, where they never had been intended to fly, caused the Air Force to call off that test after only a few missions.[4]

Frustrated by criticism of its inability to stop the infiltration flow, the Air Force tried to improve its night strike capability. Unfortunately, its only night hunters were two RB-57s with infrared sensors, and even those aircraft were still under test. In February 1966, the Air Force assigned the 433d and 479th Tactical Fighter Squadrons of the 8th Tactical Fighter Wing the sole mission of night interdiction in Laos. Their F-4C aircraft had night sensors but no real-time cockpit displays, and their forward-looking radar provided only a navigation capability. The crews had received almost no night bombing training and had little night experience, causing one of the squadron commanders to evaluate the Air Force night interdiction effort in Southeast Asia as "sporadic and ineffective."[5]

The U.S. Army in 1966 probably had a better night hunter capability than either the Air Force or the Navy. One model of the

Army's OV-1 Mohawk aircraft--the OV-1B-- carried a Motorola side-looking airborne radar with a moving target indicator capable of detecting motion down to less than 10 miles per hour radial velocity. The sensor mapped 10-nautical-mile-wide swatches on either side of the aircraft from an altitude of 5,000 feet, and the resultant imagery could be displayed to the crew in near real time, or electronically relayed to a ground station for display and recording on film. Another version of the Mohawk carried an H.B. Singer infrared sensor with a resolution of about 6 feet at 1,500 feet above ground level, but it was not as productive as the radar equipped version because rain cancelled out the infrared return. 6/ Even though night interdiction was a traditional Air Force mission, the Army was making better progress toward acquiring an effective mission capability.

Advocates of Night Interdiction

Disturbed by the inability of U.S. tactical aircraft to stem the flow of men and materiel through Laos into South Vietnam, President Lyndon B. Johnson in December 1965 asked the Air Force if it could improve its night operations. The Air Force had already contracted with the Dalmo-Victor Corporation for low light level television in four A-1E aircraft for tests in Southeast Asia. In addition, a tentative plan called for equipping a cargo aircraft with sensors and weapons for use in night interdiction. 7/ The two projects represented only a small effort, however, and the program needed additional impetus.

President Johnson next asked his science adviser, Dr. Donald F. Hornig, to investigate existing technology and potential research projects for applicability to the night air attack problem. Dr. Hornig replied that limited money had hampered research, but more rapid progress was possible with increased funding. Dr. Vincent V. McRae of Dr. Hornig's staff and Dr. Richard L. Garwin of the President's Scientific Advisory Council discussed night operations with Air Force research and development managers, including Gen. Bernard A. Schriever, commander of the Air Force Systems Command, and Lt. Gen. James Ferguson, Deputy Chief of Staff for Research and Development at Air Force headquarters.8/ The upshot of these conversations was a project labeled Shed Light.

Operation Shed Light

General Ferguson reacted to his discussions with Drs. McRae and Garwin by establishing a task force within his staff on 7 February 1966 to examine the problems associated with night attack. On 5 March, the group proposed 29 actions to improve night navigation, target acquisition, and ordnance delivery. The task force further proposed that the Air Force acquire four special aircraft: a self-contained night attack aircraft for use in lightly defended areas, a hunter aircraft to guide strike aircraft to well-defended targets, an airborne illuminator for close support night operations, and a forward air controller aircraft for use at night.9/

Once the task force conclusions were presented to the Air Staff Board, Gen. William H. Blanchard, Vice Chief of Staff, told General Ferguson on 18 March to initiate a formal project, which became Shed Light. Blanchard also told all Air Force major commands to support Shed Light fully, and invited R&D personnel from the other services to participate.10/

Air Force Systems Command then began planning for Shed Light. At the call of the System Command's Deputy for Limited War at Aeronautical Systems Division, members of Tactical Air Command, Air Force Logistics Command, and Air Training Command gathered at Wright-Patterson AFB, Ohio, and on 9 June 1966, sent to the Air Staff a proposal for nearly simultaneous R&D, aircraft modification, equipment testing, and personnel training. Having identified nine new weapons systems and 77 R&D tasks, they grouped these according to their expected contribution to night capability and the date when each should be ready for use in Southeast Asia. On 15 July, Gen. John P. McConnell, Chief of Staff, United States Air Force, a-proved the proposal " . . . for planning purposes and implementation as specific programs are directed and funds are made available."11/

To provide an Air Staff focal point, Maj. Gen. Andrew J. Evans, Director of Development, on 1 July 1966, named Col. Wirth H. Corrie as his assistant for Shed Light and gave him a staff of three. Other Air Staff managers continued to handle individual Shed Light efforts, but they reported to Colonel Corrie who, in turn, informed Generals Evans, Ferguson, and McConnell. Operation Shed Light thus became a management device to focus attention on night air attack problems and to allow key decision-makers to react quickly to crises.12/

Officials within the Department of Defense focused considerable attention upon the Air Force's night operations. In August 1966, for example, Maj. Kenneth P. Burns of the Air Staff

Plans and Operations Directorate briefed Secretary of Defense Robert S. McNamara and his staff on night operations in Southeast Asia. General Evans also explained Operation Shed Light to McNamara. When questioned by Deputy Secretary of Defense Cyrus R. Vance, General McConnell reported that the Air Force had increased its night attack sorties over North Vietnam from 506 in April to 1,935 in July. However, in the same period, sorties over Laos decreased from 637 to 376, but a decline in the number of day sorties resulted in the night sorties being a larger percentage of the total. When that percentage dropped significantly during September, Air Force headquarters reminded the Seventh Air Force, successor to the 2d Air Division, of a continuing "high level interest."13/

That same high level interest caused General McConnell's office to ask Gen. Hunter Harris, Jr., Commander-in-Chief, Pacific Air Forces, why the night attack sorties continued to decrease. General Harris replied that the divided responsibility for missions over North Vietnam and Laos prevented PACAF and the Seventh Air Force from maintaining enough flexibility in managing resources. The Air Force also lacked the sensors, aircraft, and weapons capable of accurate acquisition and destruction of vehicles at night.14/

On 24 November, Lt. Gen. William W. Momyer, Seventh Air Force commander, told General Harris that his main problem was one of finding " . . . a substitute for the eyeball which will tell the pilot where the vehicle is, how fast it is going, and when to drop his munitions for destruction." Displeased with Shed Light, General Momyer said, "The sensors we have and [those] being proposed are for [a] 120-knot force, while the requirement as dictated by the enemy is sensors for a 500-knot force."15/

Operation Shed Light slowed dramatically after General Ferguson left the Pentagon in September 1966 to assume command of the Air Force Systems Command. By year's end, General Evans agreed with Maj. Gen. Henry B. Kucheman, Jr., Aerospace Systems Division commander, that Shed Light was not moving quickly enough because its competing projects wasted time and energy. Air Force headquarters then enjoined the major commands to cooperate instead of compete, but Shed Light remained behind schedule. Further, no Shed Light aircraft had yet reached Southeast Asia.

Searching for a quick way to provide a Shed Light aircraft, the Air Force searched for one it could quickly convert to carry low light level television, laser-ranging sensors, and an automatic weapons delivery system. All of these items and more had been recommended earlier in February 1966 when civilian scientists met at Ramey Air Force Base and concluded that an increased night attack competence was more important in Vietnam for successful interdiction than was an all-weather strike capability.17/ At any rate, the Air Force finally chose the U.S. Navy's Grumman S-2, designed originally for antisubmarine warfare. The Office of the Secretary of Defense and the Navy agreed in September 1966 that the Air Force could modify two S-2D aircraft as prototypes and an additional 12 for operations as the first self-contained night attack aircraft in Southeast Asia. Despite an immediate allocation of $7 million and the full support of Dr. John S. Foster, Director of Defense Research & Engineering, and top Air Force officials, by January 1967, the Air Force Systems Command had not contracted for modification of the two prototypes even though the Navy said they were available. The Air Force finally took delivery of the two S-2Ds in May and contracted with Grumman Aircraft Corporation the following month for modification. Grumman promised the first aircraft by 31 May 1968, and the second by 30 November 1968. 18/

Secretary of the Air Force Harold Brown was well aware of the problems in night strike operations. While in Development, Research and Engineering, he had sponsored night vision research, particularly low light level television. During a visit to 2d Air Division headquarters in January 1966, Secretary Brown asked pointed questions concerning the apparent lack of initiative toward improving Air Force capabilities for night attack. Consequently, Maj. Gen. Gilbert C. Meyers, Deputy Commander of the 2d Air Division, told his staff to prepare a Southeast Asia Operational Requirement (SEAOR 35) for a self-contained night attack aircraft, one carrying every device needed to acquire and attack ground targets and totally independent of ground or airborne assistance. Citing advanced in forward looking infrared and low light level television sensors, SEAOR 35 suggested a 3-phase program beginning with a slow cargo or bomber aircraft, progressing to a small jet bomber such as the B-57, and culminating in a high performance fighter such as the F-111D. 19/

When Systems Command received SEAOR 35, the Aerospace Systems Division already was working on three projects that might partially satisfy the requirement. The first of the projects, designated Tropic Moon I, was the already mentioned installation of low light level television in A-1E aircraft; and while it had begun a test cycle, it was not expected in Vietnam before the end of 1967, if then. A second project, Lonesome Tiger, involved the installation of a forward looking infrared sensor in a B-26. It, too, had been tested, but shelved in July 1967 because the sensor range proved too limited to permit an attack on the first pass. The third project, Black Spot, called for testing a C-123 with forward looking radar, forward looking infrared and low light level television. Testing of Black Spot became entangled with the desire to install a Navy sponsored ignition detection sensor known as Black Crow; consequently by July 1967, it was not underway.[20] None of these projects met the total requirement nor did they combine multiple sensors in a jet, the final two phases called for by SEAOR 35. Still, the Air Force had hoped for some contribution, which failed to materialize.

Yet another project where the Air Force felt Brown's stinging criticism was Tropic Moon II, an effort designed to test an improved low light level television system. Brown was unhappy that by January 1967, the Air Force had not even selected an aircraft. Selection finally was made on 29 March 1967, with the decision to install the Tropic Moon II equipment in three B-57 aircraft to be sent to Southeast Asia as soon as possible. The Air Force notified all concerned commands on 12 April, and soon thereafter Westinghouse received the modification contract for the aircraft that PACAF chose and ferried from Southeast Asia to Baltimore, Maryland. By mid-1967, the Air Force estimated that the Tropic Moon II planes would be sent to Southeast Asia by late September.[21]

Meanwhile, General Momyer in April 1967 had added increased impetus to the overall Shed Light project by sending in SEAOR 117, asking for development of a more extensive line of sensors, additional weapons and aircraft, and techniques for night and all-weather interdiction of moving vehicles. Still, by mid-1967 the Air Force seemed as far as ever from having a self-contained night attack aircraft.[22]

CHAPTER II -- TROPIC MOON III

Maj. Gen. Albert W. Schinz, Tactical Air Warfare Center commander, had long advocated an improved night strike capability. He had won TAC and PACAF support by May 1967 for a General Dynamics proposal to equip fifteen B-57 aircraft with low light level television, forward looking radar, and infrared sensors under a project labeled Night Rider, but initially the Air Staff had rejected the idea as too costly and unnecessarily risky. General Schinz, however, later convinced representatives of Air Force research, testing, and operating agencies that the B-57 was the best vehicle for existing sensor technology until the Air Force could move on to the F-111D aircraft as the next self-contained night attack system. Within weeks the Air Staff directed implementation of Tropic Moon III, the conversion of B-57s to self-contained night attack configuration. 1/

Concept and Definition

Because the Air Force need for a self-contained night attack aircraft was so urgent, General Schinz proposed that Systems Command skip the conceptual and definition phases and proceed directly to acquisition.* In SEAOR 35, the 2d Air Division had specifically mentioned the B-57, which already was in use with Tropic Moon II, and the available sensors seemed to match B-57

---

*(C) AFSC Manual 375-4, System Program Management Procedures, divided a system's life cycle into four phases: conceptual--the genesis of both the technology and the need; definition--mating the technology to the need by designing a system both technically and economically feasible; acquisition--procuring and testing the system; and operational--using the system to fulfill its mission.

performance. The war in Southeast Asia would not wait, and the Air Staff advised that " . . . the urgency of need suggests departure from normal procedures . . . ." Consequently Systems Command reluctantly agreed to skip the first two phases.2/

The Air Staff then left no room for hesitation or doubt when it told Systems Command to build a prototype "immediately" for testing by September 1968, and to plan for simultaneous procurement of a full squadron of B-57s "to be deployed as soon as possible." The Southeast Asia Projects Division wanted a plan for the prototype within 2 weeks and a procurement plan within a month. The B-57 aircraft would carry forward looking radar with terrain warning and moving target indicator features, low light level television, and forward looking infrared if such a sensor could be installed. Systems Command's reaction to the task was hardly optimistic. Maj. Gen. Joseph J. Cody, Jr., Systems Command's Chief of Staff, noted, "Here we go again. I wonder if anyone thought of describing the environment/state-of-the-art and then asking the developer to accomplish design." Within a week, however, Systems Command asked Air Force headquarters to select a B-57 for the prototype Tropic Moon III aircraft. By the end of October 1967, an Aerospace Systems Division task force--with augmentation from Air Force headquarters, Tactical Air Command and Systems Command--submitted its plan for a prototype aircraft.3/

A further step took place when TAC on 7 November 1967 issued Required Operational Commitment 62-67 calling for a night attack wing composed of three squadrons of B-57s and a composite Shed Light squadron of NC-123, RC-130, S-2D, and A-1E aircraft. TAC reasserted General Schinz's argument that earlier Shed Light aircraft were too slow, carried too few munitions, lacked growth potential, and were not able to detect targets at long range or attack well defended targets. The B-57 aircraft were available, had room for several sensors, and could carry 9,000 pounds of bombs at speeds of 160 to 500 knots. On 8 November, Systems Command told the Aerospace Systems Division to be ready for immediate action when the Air Staff released funds for Tropic Moon III, and to prepare a Request for Proposal--the document used to solicit bids from contractors--assuming a fixed-price contract and incentives for both bombing accuracy and early delivery. The Systems Division also was to prepare a procurement plan by 20 November 1967.4/

As the Aerospace Systems Division developed its procurement plan, it also briefed key officials on the Tropic Moon III project and solicited their support. Following a 28 November Air Staff Board recommendation, General McConnell approved the modification of sixteen B-57 aircraft and Secretary Brown authorized reprogramming to shift the required funds from other Air Force projects. For an estimated $51.99 million, the Systems Division expected to put sixteen Tropic Moon III B-57s into combat by April 1969.5/

Meanwhile, Gunship II, an AC-130 equipped with 7.62mm and 20mm guns, already in Southeast Asia for testing, had proved itself an effective truck killer and provided a potential yardstick for evaluating Tropic Moon III. The Southeast Asia Projects Division commissioned Analytic Services, Inc. (ANSER) to compare the two. Based on ANSER's model, Tropic Moon III would have " . . . a better than 2 to 1 cost advantage . . . ," an advantage that the Southeast Asia Projects Division staff had failed to exploit fully. Instead, they had stressed Tropic Moon III's survivability where enemy defenses were too concentrated or effective for Gunship II missions, arguing for a mixed force of Gunship II and Tropic Moon III planes rather than Tropic Moon III as a replacement for Gunship II. The most spectacular staff claim was that: "Considering the present North Vietnamese truck inventory and their replacement rate during 1966, the Tropic Moon III force could reduce this inventory to between 40 and 50 percent of its present level in 6 months of operation."6/

The stated primary mission of the Tropic Moon III aircraft was to restrict the enemy's ability to move and support his forces during darkness. The Tropic Moon III aircrews would fly at night along enemy lines of communications to detect and destroy moving vehicles, shipping on rivers and canals, and some selected stationary targets as small as jeeps. As a self-contained night attack aircraft, Tropic Moon III would carry appropriate sensors and weapons to enable it to find and destroy targets at night on the first pass without the use of visible artificial illumination. The term "self-contained" did not exclude the use of ground-based navigation systems, such as long range navigation (LORAN), but encouraged the inclusion of on-board navigation systems for long-range interdiction missions.7/

Because the Gunship II prototype had been so successful on interdiction missions in SEA, Secretary Brown in November 1967 authorized the conversion of seven additional C-130s to gunships. Shortly thereafter, on 12 December, the three Tropic Moon II B-57s reached Phan Rang Air Base, South Vietnam, and four crated Tropic Moon I A-1Es left California by ship on 22 December. Shed Light projects finally began showing some progress.8/

The Statement of Work

When the Aerospace Systems Division advertised for bids on 8 March 1968, it provided a detailed description of the Tropic Moon III mission, operational profile, equipment, and sensor specifications. In effect, the Air Force offered the final definition of what its designers thought Tropic Moon III should be, thus providing a base for measuring the actual program and eventual aircraft performance.9/

Basically, the Air Force required the potential Tropic Moon III contractor to modifiy government-furnished B-57Bs to a new "G" configuration by integrating government- and contractor-furnished equipment. Besides the basic airframe, the Air Force would furnish engines, electronic countermeasures equipment, and communications sets. The contractor would provide the weapons delivery and navigation systems and modify the airframes. Aerospace Systems Division's C-141/C-130 Systems Project Office would manage the contract, and the Warner Robins Air Materiel Area would furnish logistics support.10/

To further guide contractor planning, the Air Force described a typical Tropic Moon III mission. The crew would first use tactical air navigation (TACAN) and doppler navigation equipment to position their aircraft. While the pilot flew along roads or water ways at 250 knots at 500 to 5,000 feet above ground level, the sensor operator would use the forward looking radar and its moving target indicator feature to detect targets. Once a target appeared on the radar scope, the sensor operator would switch to low light level television or to forward looking infrared to identify the target and activated the automatic weapon delivery system. The sensor

B-57G EQUIPMENT LAYOUT

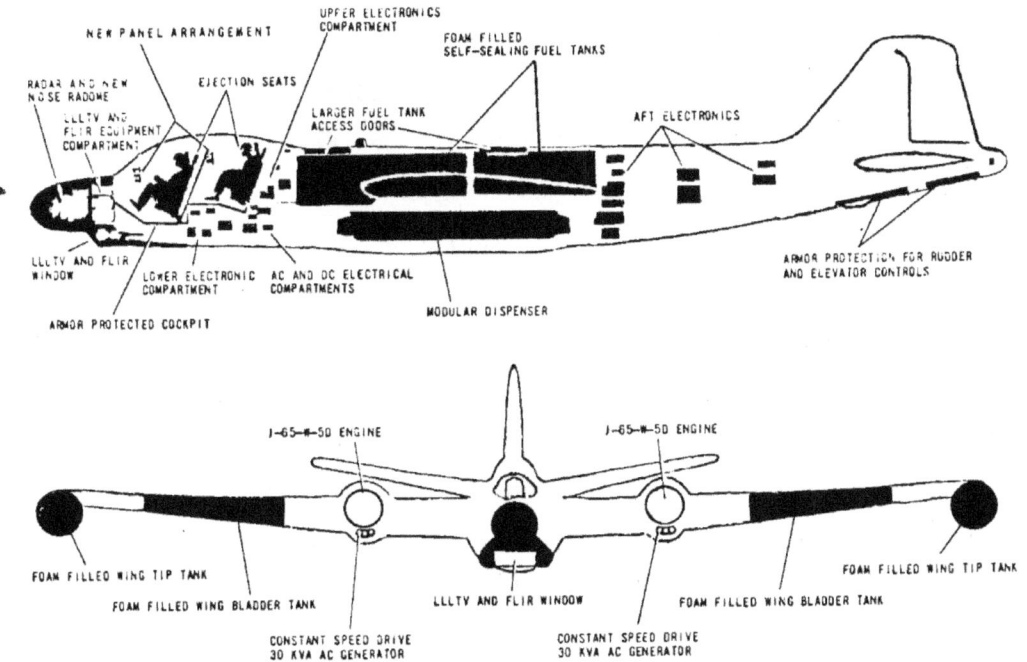

operator could track the target manually, or the sensor-computer combination could do it automatically. The sensor operator would then select the ordnance and the computer would release it at the proper moment. The pilot could make a second automatic pass, using the doppler navigation equipment and the computer to position the aircraft and release the ordnance. Each significant segment of the delivery sequence would include a manual override feature.11/

Also established were specific yardsticks for Tropic Moon III's avionics. The forward looking radar would be the equivalent of the Ling-Temco-Vought AN/APQ-126, designed for the A-7 aircraft, which included circuitry to warn of obstacles, guide the pilot along terrain contours, and display a map of the ground. The Tropic Moon III contractor would add a moving target indicator to the AN/APQ-126 capabilities. The Air Force specified the Westinghouse WX-31366 tube for the low light level television, and included highly detailed technical specifications for the forward looking infrared sensor, the weapons delivery computer, and the laser ranging sensor. The weapons delivery computer had to achieve 97- to 190-foot circular error probable from 2,000 to 3,000 feet with medium or low drag bombs. The navigation system had to be accurate to 1 percent of the distance traveled and had to include a heading-vertical reference set, doppler radar, radar altimeter usable to 5,000 feet above ground level, and a navigation computer. The electronic countermeasures equipment provided by the Air Force would include passive electronic countermeasures to interfere with enemy radar and missile guidance signals.12/

As specified, the Air Force would furnish more powerful turbojet engines to increase the B-57's speed and improve its overall performance. The contractor would provide two 30 KVA generators to augment the electrical system, air-condition the crew and electronics compartments, install polyurethane foam material in all fuel tanks for greater safety, mount self-sealing fuel tanks in the fuselage, and install armored or self-sealing fuel lines wherever a single hit could stop the flow of fuel to both engines. Additional armor plate and new ejection seats increased crew protection.13/

Funding Problems

Throughout early 1968 the Air Force actively searched for funds to speed up Tropic Moon III. Events in Southeast Asia assuredly enhanced the importance of a self-contained night attack aircraft, but the funds continued to be scarce. On 12 February 1968, Secretary Brown asked the Department of Defense to allow the Air Force to reprogram $54 million; and on 24 February, Deputy Secretary of Defense Paul H. Nitze approved the request.14/

When it subsequently decided that it could reprogram only half of the cost of Tropic Moon III, the Air Staff asked for an additional appropriation to cover the other half. Mr. Nitze disapproved any additional specific funds, but he added $25 million to the overall Air Force budget for fleet modification. In effect, this left a loophole through which the Air Force could draw funds to reconfigure the B-57G to perform new missions. In early April General Dynamics, Ling-Temco-Vought, North American Rockwell, and Westinghouse submitted bids, all at least $30 million higher than the original $52 million Air Force estimate. On 8 May 1968, Maj. Gen. William G. Moore, Director of Operational Requirements and Development Plans, authorized $51,269,650 for reconfiguring sixteen B-57s--$6.3 million for the prototype and $2.5 million for each production aircraft. But that same day, General Ferguson stopped all Tropic Moon III actions.15/

Although General Ferguson cited the money shortage as the primary reason for the program halt, growing opposition to the Shed Light program's orientation also played a major role. The program to convert the Navy S-2Ds to self-contained night attack aircraft had come to a halt in January 1968 after TAC, PACAF, and the Seventh Air Force complained that the S-2D was too slow for the mission and too vulnerable to anti-aircraft fire. Because the low light level television system in the Tropic Moon I A-1E aircraft was obsolete before it was sent to Southeast Asia, that program would not go beyond the four test aircraft. Most disappointing of all was the poor showing of the Tropic Moon II B-57s in Southeast Asia. In 182 combat sorties, they detected 456 trucks but destroyed or damaged only 39. Gen. John D. Ryan, CINCPACAF, told his staff, "I am tired of us buying everything they send us. We have a marginal system here and are up against the manpower ceiling. Draft me a message to 7th telling General Momyer I want to return this thing to CONUS [continental United States]." In March, General Momyer had complained to General Ferguson that the Tropic Moon II low light level television system could not find targets early enough to attack on the first pass, its field of view was too narrow for easy recognition, and its navigation system was unreliable. In reply, General Ferguson had emphasized Tropic Moon III's multiple sensors, particularly the long-range forward looking radar and the improved navigation system to be installed in the B-57Gs.16/ The program, however, was at a standstill.

During May and June 1968, everyone tried desperately to get Tropic Moon III moving. The contractors even trimmed their modification proposals, but all of the bids remained well over the Air Force estimates. When all possible avenues of financial aid had been explored without success, the Air Force found itself faced with three possible alternatives: (1) reduce the capability of the 16 programmed aircraft, (2) modify fewer than 16 aircraft, or (3) eliminate some contractor responsibilities. If forced to make such a difficult choice, PACAF and the Seventh Air Force wanted fewer aircraft will full capability, but they and TAC continued to hope for a full program. The Air Staff Board decided instead to save some money by approving the Aeronautical Systems Division's proposal to reduce the force capability. 17/

Having decided to proceed with the full program of 16 aircraft but with reduced capability, the Air Staff switched Class V modification funds to Tropic Moon III. Lt. Gen. Joseph R. Holzapple, Deputy Chief of Staff for Research and Development at Air Force headquarters, tentatively approved the 16 aircraft program, and General McConnell made it final on 29 June. 18/

General Ferguson, however, wanted to give General Momyer, the user, one last chance to veto the project: "While I am anxious to move out as rapidly as possible, I would not want to do so if you believe the system to be unsatisfactory. If this is the case, I suggest you inform HQ USAF in sufficient time to preclude the unnecessary expenditures of funds." General Momyer earlier had expressed misgivings about the entire program but now withdrew his opposition, the final obstacle to signing the contract. Westinghouse Electric

Corporation of Baltimore, Maryland, on 15 July 1968, agreed to modify sixteen B-57s to the Tropic Moon III B-57G configuration for $78.3 million.19/

CHAPTER III -- THE B-57G

Ironically, the Air Force bought the aircraft chosen for conversion to a self-contained night attack configuration during the early 1950s for use as a night intruder. As noted earlier, at the outbreak of the Korean War, the only light bomber in the Air Force was the obsolete B-26, marginally effective during daylight but lacking the necessary equipment for night combat. After considering a number of proposals and evaluating several aircraft, the Air Proving Ground Command* recommended that the United States manufacture the English Electric Canberra jet bomber used in the Royal Air Force. The Air Force Senior Officers Board approved the proposal and recommended that the aircraft go directly into production to provide a night intruder capability at the earliest possible date. The Canberra, designated the B-57, entered the Air Force inventory as an off-the-shelf aircraft without experimental or test models. On 2 March 1951, Air Force headquarters told the Air Materiel Command--later the Air Force Logistics Command--to negotiate a contract with the Glenn L. Martin Company for the production of 250 B-57 aircraft for use in the Korean War.

The B-57B

Despite the Air Force Senior Officers Board's determination that there would be only minimal changes in the Canberra, some

---
* Later Air Proving Ground Center at Eglin AFB, Florida.

alterations proved necessary to bring the aircraft up to U.S. standards. The U.S. Air Force changed the fuel system, cockpit canopy, bomb bay, and gun installations to use U.S. equipment; altered material specifications, fabrication tolerances, and metal gauges to U.S. criteria; and redesigned electrical wiring to meet U.S. requirements. Because of recurring problems with the Rolls Royce Avon jet engines in the Canberra, Martin used the Wright Aeronautical Company's J-65 turbojet engines. Martin also installed a new rotary bomb bay door that made high speed bombing possible. The installation of U.S. electronic equipment completed the basic changes, and the new aircraft became the B-57A. Only eight were produced.

Because of an urgent need for a fast reconnaissance aircraft to replace the RB-26, the Air Force had Martin remove all guns and associated equipment and mount aerial cameras and appropriate controls to produce a reconnaissance version of the B-57A, the RB-57A. Lighter by several hundred pounds than the bomber version, the reconnaissance model could operate from short runways, but had no provision for inflight refueling. Also, structural flutter limited its top speed to about Mach 0.75. The Air Force ordered 67 RB-57A reconnaissance aircraft, the first of which flew in October 1953. Intended as an interim replacement for the RB-26, the RB-57A was not an all-weather aircraft and evidenced only moderate speed improvement over the older aircraft. The aircraft would undergo some five nomenclature changes plus hundreds of modifications to achieve its B-57G status.*/

Eighteen Months of Delays

Based at Johnson Air Base in Japan for some time, the 8th and 13th Bomber Squadrons, Tactical, in January 1965 moved their B-57s to Clark Air Base in the Phillipines for possible action in Southeast Asia. Small numbers of the aircraft flew missions from Bien Hoa and Da Nang Air Bases in South Vietnam, but PACAF eventually inactivated both squadrons. The Air Force chose the 13th as the unit to test the B-57G in Southeast Asia and flew selected B-57C aircraft from Clark Air Base to Baltimore for conversion to the Tropic Moon III configuration.

(U) Once the contracts were let, Tropic Moon III followed standard Air Force procurement procedures. Martin first repaired

---

* Air Force pilots were most unhappy with the arrangement of the Canberra cockpit area. The pilot sat in the upper left half of the cockpit, with the bombardier-navigator awkwardly positioned below him and to his right rear. A complete cockpit redesign placed the B-57 crew members in tandem under a centrally aligned canopy and deleted the Plexiglas nose through which the Canberra bombardier operated his bombsight. The conversion produced the B-57B, which became the standard and most numerous of all the models. With the addition of dual controls in the rear seat, the B-57B became the B-57C, the trainer version of the light jet bomber. Adding photographic equipment plus mating huge new wings and new engines to a B-57A fuselage produced the RB-57D, a specialized, extremely high-altitude reconnaissance and research aircraft. Installation of tow-target reels and associated equipment transformed a limited number of B-57C aircraft into B-57E models. 1/ Modification of fifteen B-57B and B-57C aircraft for high-altitude air sampling missions produced the RB-57F, a highly specialized aircraft of limited capability. 2/ Sixteen B-57Bs modified to self-contained night attack configuration became B-57Gs.

and modernized each of the selected airframes to bring it up to existing standards, and then delivered them to the Westinghouse factory for B-57G modification.

(U) Air Force Systems Command monitored the modification, Logistics Command provided logistic support, Tactical Air Command trained the aircrews, and Air Force headquarters coordinated the entire program. The normal three-phase testing program was prescribed, with separate aircraft designated for each phase. Category I testing, conducted by Westinghouse, assured that the contractor had provided an aircraft capable of carrying out the intended mission. Category II testing, carried out by Systems Command, made certain that the aircraft met Air Force operational requirements. Category III testing by Tactical Air Command measured the operational capability of the new aircraft and developed necessary tactics for its use.

(U) Systems Command delegated Category II responsibilities to its Armament Development and Test Center at Eglin AFB, Florida, and TAC assigned its Category III test responsibilities to the Tactical Air Warfare Center at the same base. Because the U.S. Navy had cognizance of the Westinghouse factory in Baltimore, Navy personnel administered the contract, accepting the B-57Gs from Westinghouse and turning them over to the Aeronautical Systems Division and and TAC. The Aeronautical Systems Division purchased unique aerospace ground equipment and spare parts for Categories I and II testing, while the Warner-Robins Air Materiel Area, responsible for all Logistics Command B-57 support, procured aerospace ground equipment and spare parts for Category III tests and normal operations. It was an involved but effective system that had worked many times before.

Tropic Moon III moved smoothly through the first few months of the contract, seemingly without difficulty. On 14 August 1968, General Moore allocated $14.6 million for the prototype and $3.3 million for each of the 15 production aircraft, plus money for spare parts that brought the total contract cost to $78.3 million. Martin began work on the first two B-57Bs in August 1968, and turned them over to Westinghouse before the end of the month. By January 1969, Westinghouse was working on 11 airframes and Martin was modernizing the remainder.

Meanwhile, the systems project office steered the project through conferences on design, ground equipment, training, handbooks, and munitions. Air Force headquarters moved B-57 combat crew training from Clark Air Base to MacDill AFB, Florida. Air Force Systems Command planned to test the new Hayes bomb dispenser on the rotary bomb bay door of the B-57G. In November 1968, the project office predicted that Tropic Moon III would reach Southeast Asia in December 1969, early enough to take part in the next Laotian interdiction campaign.3/ Anticipating rapid progress, Tactical Air Command on 8 February 1969 reactivated the 13th Bombardment Squadron, Tactical, to fly the B-57G, and assigned it to the 15th Tactical Fighter Wing at MacDill Air Force Base pending use in combat.4/ It appeared that Tropic Moon III was on schedule.

Appearances, however, were deceiving. Recurring sensor problems made it obvious by late March 1969 that the B-57G was well behind schedule and could not possibly be ready for combat by December. Maj. Gen. John L. Zoeckler, Deputy Chief of Staff for Systems at Systems Command on 21 April formally asked Air Force headquarters to approve a 6-month delay in deploying the B-57G squadron. Representatives of all concerned commands and agencies agreed on 5 June, and the Air Staff approved a new deployment date of June 1970.5/

Although the slippage of the deployment date generated no formal change in the B-57G mission, there appeared to be some change in the Air Force attitude toward the system. In April 1969, Dr. Foster asked the Assistant Secretaries for research and development of the Army, Navy, and Air Force to describe each service's efforts to improve its night air operational capability. The Air Force stressed the emphasis being placed on sensor technology and described the B-57G as " . . . one of the Air Force's largest efforts toward creating a weapon system specifically tailored to night and limited adverse weather attack . . . ." A year earlier, the Air Force had emphasized the combat potential of the B-57G in its truck killing role, but as the delays continued, the Air Force seemed to be thinking of the B-57G as a test vehicle declaring that:

> The B-57G program itself, however important it is, is only an evolutionary step in the ultimate development of a high-speed, fully integrated, self-contained night/all-weather weapon system. The Air Force's approach is to draw on the technology and operational lessons of programs like the B-57G and the F-111D with its Mk II avionics, to arrive at an effective weapon delivery system for the inventory aircraft.6/

Even though the June 1970 deployment date apparently allowed ample time for completing the modification and testing the aircraft, further setbacks soon threatened even that date.

Texas Instruments fell further behind in deliveries of its forward looking infrared sensor, causing Westinghouse to slow its conversion effort. Then too, the Air Force was late with shipments of ground equipment for the Category I tests. Tests of the Hayes dispenser and the development of new cluster bombs were delayed. To make matters worse, on 15 July Westinghouse announced a projected cost overrun of $3.5 million, even without delays.

Westinghouse finally began Category I testing on 18 July 1969, 3 days behind the latest schedule, and by mid-August had fallen behind even more because Texas Instruments had delivered only three forward looking infrared sensors. Gambling on future program improvement, the systems project office in September decided to begin Category II tests before completion of Category I.

About the same time, a working group began planning for B-57G munitions, including the laser guided bombs that the Air Force hoped to use. The Air Force on 28 October accepted on an interim basis those aircraft that were ready for Category II tests, and planned to begin testing as quickly as trained aircrews became available. 7/

By November, Col. William Y. Smith, Military Assistant to the Secretary of the Air Force, was able to tell Secretary Robert Seamans that the B-57G program seemed to have regained its momentum. Colonel Smith blamed production delays on the need for contractor redesign of the forward looking infrared sensor and Air Force tardiness in delivering the electronic countermeasures equipment. However, the revised schedule appeared to provide adequate time for developing and testing all components.

Just as things seemed to be moving smoothly at last, an aircraft accident ended all hope of meeting the June deployment date. The systems project office had planned to use four aircraft on an interim basis for Category II and munitions testing, but on 8 December 1969, Westinghouse pointed out that they could not update those aircraft for final acceptance if the Air Force was to test them 1,500 miles away. While this problem was being discussed, one aircraft (No. 53-3905) crashed into the Sassafras River near Baltimore on 6 December, killing both Martin crew members. The loss was a severe jolt because the aircraft had been scheduled to join the Category II test force as soon as Westinghouse released it. Faced with further delays, the project office called a program review conference.9/

When the B-57G program managers met at Wright-Patterson Air Force Base on 22 January 1970, the situation seemed worse than ever. Bad weather continued to prevent completion of both Category I test flights in Baltimore and Category II flights in Florida. Category III test flights had not begun, nor had munitions tests. The 13th Bombardment Squadron, Tactical, was training with B-57C and B-57E aircraft, but without the B-57G special sensors they accomplished little. The systems project office expected the first operational B-57G to be ready by March and the remainder by June, but that schedule obviously left no time for training the aircrews for a June deployment. The project office stated that it would be necessary to slip the deployment date, and Air Force headquarters on 11 March announced that the B-57G would deploy to Southeast Asia in September 1970, a further delay of 3 months.10/

Testing, Training, and Problems

September 1970 became a firm deployment date and everyone struggled to meet it. The Armament Development and Test Center performed Category II and munitions compatibility tests while the Tactical Air Warfare Center carried out Category III tests and the 15th Tactical Fighter Wing's 4424th Combat Crew Training Squadron trained the B-57G aircrews. When Categories II and III tests revealed major deficiencies in the performance of the forward looking radar, TAC and the Air Force Systems Command proposed a further deployment delay, but the Air Force Chief of Staff was adamant--the B-57G would enter combat in September.

But even the firm stand of the Chief of Staff was not enough to keep the program on schedule. When the program managers met on 14 April, they admitted that the program was far behind schedule. Westinghouse had finished Category I and the Air Force had begun munitions tests, but the Armament Development and Test Center had completed only 22 of the 45 Category II tests. Further, the Tactical Air Warfare Center had only recently received two of the three aircraft needed for Category III tests.

According to the systems project office, Westinghouse was four aircraft behind schedule because assembly line modifications lacked the quality of those of the prototype, and the original design engineers, already assigned to other programs, were not available to solve the problems that arose. In addition, Westinghouse had tried to cut corners by omitting post installation tests on certain doubtful components, especially computers. Air Force inspectors rejected those aircraft with faulty equipment, as expected, forcing the contractor to repair the unsatisfactory components and to repeat the acceptance tests.

The program managers on 14 April altered the schedule to allow Westinghouse to deliver the aircraft in groups within the overall deadlines established in January, rather than individually by specific dates. They also learned that the ferry range of the fully equipped B-57G was much shorter than expected. With the modified nose and the added sensors and electronic equipment, the aircraft was so heavy and slow that it could not possibly fly across the Pacific Ocean.

Within a month, Westinghouse had fallen even farther behind schedule as it had diverted production technicians to find and correct malfunctions in electronic components. The Armament Development and Test Center, faced with a deadline of 22 April for completion of Category II, flew two B-57Gs 7 days a week, but was unable to meet the suspense date. On 6 May, the test center agreed to continue Category II with one of the B-57Gs while returning the second aircraft to Westinghouse for removal of the test instrumentation. Every available aircraft had to be made operational, particularly after TAC announced that it needed twelve B-57Gs before the end of June if it was to complete combat crew training on time. 12/

Munitions tests, completed by the test center in May, demonstrated that the B-57G could deliver 500-pound Mk-82 and 750-pound M-117 conventional bombs and the M-36E1 fire bomb. The Hayes dispenser proved compatible. Test missions by a B-57E showed that the laser guided bombs could hit stationary targets when dropped at the relatively slow speed of the B-57G. With munitions testing largely completed, Category III tests began on 29 April. 13/

About this same time, logistics problems threatened the entire project. Proceeding under the belief that the B-57G was only a test-bed for equipment that would be tested and removed for later installation in another type of aircraft, Warner-Robins Air Materiel Area had ordered only enough spare parts for a 6-month combat evaluation. When Warner-Robins learned in May 1969 that the B-57G was to be an operational truck killer for an indefinite period, supply personnel hurriedly ordered additional spare parts. A year later, however, the original delay in requisitioning continued to cause a shortage of many essential spare parts. To further complicate the shortages, each time the contractor changed any avionics, he also altered the spare parts requirements, creating new shortages and delays.14/

Although responsible for providing aerospace ground equipment for all B-57G testing and operational evaluation, the Air Force had in fact furnished only two sets. By May 1970, Westinghouse was modifying aircraft in Baltimore, the Tactical Air Warfare Center and the Armament Development and Test Center were testing B-57Gs at Eglin Air Force Base, and the 13th Bombardment Squadron was ready to begin training at MacDill Air Force Base once it received aircraft. Two sets of ground equipment for three widely separated locations meant that one site would have to improvise.15/

Possibly as a result of Air Force threats to invoke contractual penalties for late delivery, Westinghouse delivered four B-57Gs at the end of May. Lt. Col. Paul R. Pitt, Commander of the 13th Bombardment Squadron flew the first B-57G to MacDill Air Force Base, and the squadron began training on 26 May. By 8 June, the Tactical Air Warfare Center was using three B-57Gs to develop

B-57G (FOUR VIEWS)

tactics, the squadron trained with five, the Armament Development and Test Center continued Category II testing with one, and Westinghouse continued work on the remaining six.16/

Ferry range limitations continued to be a problem as the squadron neared deployment. TAC wanted to increase the B-57G range by redesigning the nose and chin to reduce drag caused by the sensors, but the necessary engineering and contracting would take months. The systems project office recommended removing all sensors and nonessential components for shipment to Southeast Asia aboard cargo aircraft. Special teams could be sent to the overseas base to reinstall the components and sensors, and ready the B-57Gs for combat.17/

As Categories II and III testing progressed, other serious deficiencies appeared. Category III testing did not end formally until 27 July, and Category II testing finished on 28 September 1970, but as early as May the program managers set about trying to resolve arising problems. The Tactical Air Warfare Center and the Armament Development and Test Center agreed that the B-57G could carry out the self-contained night attack mission from detecting and tracking targets to automatically delivering weapons, but the installed forward looking radar, the low light level television, and the weapon delivery computer failed repeatedly after a very few hours of operation.

When Category II tests uncovered weak performance in the forward looking radar's ground map, terrain following/avoidance, and moving target indicator modes. Texas Instruments hurriedly reconfigured, tested, and reinstalled a system in the Category II aircraft. The modification improved the ground mapping presentation and seemed to solve the problems in the terrain following/avoidance equipment, but did not improve the moving target indicator mode. Over the succeeding months, Texas Instruments engineers tried several other changes but were unable to make the moving target indicator work.

MEAN TIME BETWEEN EQUIPMENT FAILURE			
	(HOURS) Category II*	Category III**	Combat Evaluation***
Forward looking radar	2.6	3.7	2.8
Low light level TV	6.05	4.6	6.2
Forward looking infrared	11.8	8.8	7.1
Navigation equipment	5.1	12.9	4.6

*ADTC, B-57 Category II Test (June 1977), pp. 73, 75, 76, 78.
**TAWC, B-57G Program Category III Test, January 1971, p. 13.
***TAWC, B-57G Combat Evaluation, March 1971, p. 19.

Early in June 1970, Westinghouse stopped installing the Texas Instruments modifications, claiming that the work was beyond their contractual obligations. Following a meeting with the systems project office on 11 June, however, Westinghouse resumed modification installation, reserving the right to charge the government for the added work.18/

Even without the threatened new charges, however, an earlier prediction of a $3.5 million cost overrun proved conservative. The lengthening delays in modification and the growing number of design changes and "fixes" raised the cost significantly. In June 1970, Westinghouse announced a cost overrun of $4.95 million, and warned that continued delays and changes might cause further increases.19/

As serious as the money problems appeared to be, the technical problems proved far more difficult to solve. The terrain following/avoidance feature of the forward looking radar proved so unreliable during Category III testing that the Tactical Air Warfare Center recommended use only under visual flight rules conditions. Since the moving target indicator did not work at all, the sensor operators had to use the low light level television and forward looking infrared sensors to find targets. The range of the television was about 5 nautical miles, while that of the infrared sensor was only 3 nautical miles, less than 1 minute of B-57G flying time. In that short time, it was impossible for the sensor operator to recognize the target, establish automatic tracking, and activate the weapon delivery computer for a first pass attack. The Tactical Air Warfare Center found that the B-57G could successfully reattack about 80 percent of such targets, but the initial pass alerted the enemy and gave him time to take evasive action or to activate his defenses.20/

Possibly the most outspoken of the critics, crew members found much to denounce in the B-57G. Maj. Douglas J. Kosan, a G-57G sensor operator, wrote a highly critical analysis of sensor performance during Category III testing. He claimed that the forward looking radar was "fair at best," and judged the low light level television effective only in clear air with at least a one-third moon. Major Kosan said he was able to find targets with the forward looking infrared sensor only if he knew their exact position before beginning his attack. Other crew members were equally critical, emphasizing the need for immediate corrective action.21/

Seeing that the program was making little progress and time was running out, General Momyer, now Tactical Air Command commander, called a conference which met at TAC headquarters on

9 July. Westinghouse agreed to rush delivery of the three additional B-57Gs needed for crew training and to expedite repair of the forward looking radar. General Ferguson decided that once Category III tests had been completed, he would move all Category II activity to MacDill Air Force Base to ease the aerospace ground equipment shortage. He also proposed weekly meetings of senior staff officers from Systems, Tactical Air, and Logistics Commands to expedite decision making and problem solution.*/ Despite General Momyer's argument that it would be best to wait until the next dry season in Laos to deploy completely ready aircraft,22/ General Ryan refused to delay further. He said: "As long as a possibility exists to make the IOC (initial operating capability) on or about 15 September, we must continue to target for it."23/ The pressure was on and time was growing short.

Deployment Preparations

As the day of decision neared, the 13th Bombardment Squadron, Tactical, had received 11 aircraft, but it could not complete all the required training by 4 September. The forward looking infrared sensor worked more dependably, but there appeared to be no improvement in the low light level television capability. The forward looking radar was not working well, and there was no significant increase in spare parts availability.24/

---

*   Complying with General Ferguson's desire for weekly meetings of senior officers from the various commands and agencies involved in the B-57G project, a group of officers first met at MacDill Air Force Base on 21 July 1970. This group's actions produced quick solutions to many problems and expedited the deployment preparations.25/

General Momyer on 10 August expressed disappointment because the B-57G was not as effective as originally expected. Even more important, in his opinion, the Air Force appeared unable to manage this major weapon system and looked "particularly suspect in the face of the many statements we all have made regarding improved systems management."26/ Asserting that it was blameless for the delays and difficulties, Air Force Systems Command pointed out that Air Staff personnel had selected the system components, organized the schedule, and determined the cost base.27/

Faced with General Ryan's determination that the Air Force would meet its announced deadline, a group of senior officers on 13 August decided that the B-57Gs would deploy in September--ready or not! The outlook was hopeful, particularly where it pertained to sensor and spare parts matters. The Air Force solved the ferry range problem on 19 August by simply directing the removal of 2,380 pounds of sensor and laser components to lighten the aircraft for an increased fuel load and better performance. In addition, Systems Command directed a 10-man team from its Aeronautical Systems Division and Westinghouse to go to the Royal Thai Air Force Base at Ubon to help the six contractor field representatives reinstall the equipment. The final "go/no-go" decision would be made on 1 September 1970.28/

Following a 1 September review of the program, General Momyer; Gen. Jack G. Merrell, Logistics Command commander; and Lt. Gen. John W. O'Neill, Systems Command Vice Commander, recommended that the 13th Bombardment Squadron leave for Southeast Asia on 15 September. The unit was approaching combat readiness, the forward looking infrared sensor and low light level television were improved, the manufacturer was predicting better moving target indicator results, and spare parts were pouring in. Noting that the aircraft performance was nearing that originally specified, General Ryan ordered the squadron to move to Ubon on 15 September. Only 11 of the fifteen B-57G aircraft would go, leaving three at MacDill Air Force Base for training replacement crews and one to complete Category II and to serve as a test-bed for improvement efforts.29/

CHAPTER IV -- IMPROVEMENT EFFORTS

Almost 3 years after it began the Shed Light program, the Air Force had sent into combat a squadron of self-contained night attack aircraft, even though those aircraft would be unable to accomplish their assigned mission unless their sensors were improved further. Having committed the B-57G to combat with a full awareness of its shortcomings, the Air Force continued its efforts to improve the sensors and other electronic components and to make changes in the airframe in order that the aircraft and its systems eventually might meet operational requirements.

Forward Looking Radar

Probably the most essential of the sensors, the forward looking radar had been most disappointing from the very beginning. Operational use of the B-57Gs revealed some of the reasons for the deficiencies. The combined Aeronautical Systems Division/Westinghouse team which reinstalled the equipment discovered that none of the magnetrons met the specified power output requirements. When the team returned to the United States, two engineers remained at Ubon to try to solve the problem, but they were unsuccessful. On 3 November 1970, the 8th Tactical Fighter Wing, to which the B-57G squadron was assigned, notified the Thirteenth Air Force that the inoperative radar sets were causing most of the B-57G missions to fail. PACAF notified Systems Command, the Systems Division, Logistics Command, and Warner-Robins Air Materiel Area that the radar suffered not only from weak magnetrons but also from tuning problems with local oscillators and arcing in the waveguides.[1/]

Even as PACAF alerted the commands, the systems project office discovered that Texas Instruments was not using the specified Raytheon magnetrons. Instead, the company was limiting the sweep on magnetrons produced by Litton Industries for other radar sets, and then assigning to those modified magnetrons the stock numbers intended for the AN/APQ-139 magnetrons. As soon as the substitution was discovered, Texas Instruments procured five new magnetrons from Raytheon and sent them to Ubon. The new magnetrons, however, did not provide the required power. The 13th Bombardment Squadron tried detecting targets with the low light level television or the forward looking infrared sensor and then using the moving target indicator to spot them on radar, but to no avail; the moving target indicator feature remained inoperative and useless.2/

Texas Instruments in December 1970 reported that the forward looking radar " . . . provides satisfactory performance to fulfill the mission objectives in SEA," but Air Force records refuted that claim. A Warner-Robins official blamed Westinghouse whose contract required them to produce an effective forward looking radar. The Air Force Director of Maintenance Engineering said the hurried deployment had resulted in reduced quality control in the modification and an absence of required technical data. The Aeronautical Systems Division agreed that the "crash program" had resulted in reduced quality control, but added that Category I testing had ended before moving target indicator, radar bombing, and navigation capabilities had been tested. The Systems Division also contended that the sensors could have been improved further with time, but that the Laos dry season and the North Vietnamese resupply campaign would not wait.3/

Aware that a quick fix for the radar was not possible, Systems Command called a meeting of the commands involved to develop a program to produce an operational radar set. Representatives of Air Force headquarters, Systems, Logistics, and Tactical Air Commands, and PACAF on 15 December 1970 concluded that the Air Force could either institute a massive remedial program for the forward looking radar, purchase an entirely new radar, or remove the radar from the B-57Gs. A week later, Systems Command told the systems project office to develop a remedial program, having chosen that alternative as the one that would probably produce the desired results in the shortest time. PACAF agreed to remove one of the AN/APQ-139 radars from a B-57G at Ubon and return it to Texas Instruments for the remedial program. 4/

The Systems Division also asked Westinghouse to contribute its ideas for the remedial program, calling upon its experience in the modification process. On 5 January 1971, the systems project office submitted a plan to establish forward looking radar baseline performance on the Category II aircraft at Eglin Air Force Base as part of the remedial action. On 13 and 14 January, all commands reviewed the program; General Ryan then approved it, and on 9 February the Aeronautical Systems Division was authorized to spend the necessary $2 million. 5/

Through the spring of 1971, Texas Instruments redesigned the components and the Armament Development and Test Center tested the radar. On 13 and 14 May, the Aeronautical Systems Division summarized the continuing problem as strobing, poor ground mapping, and loss of video above 10,000 feet above ground level, caused by low output power, moisture and low air pressure in the waveguide,

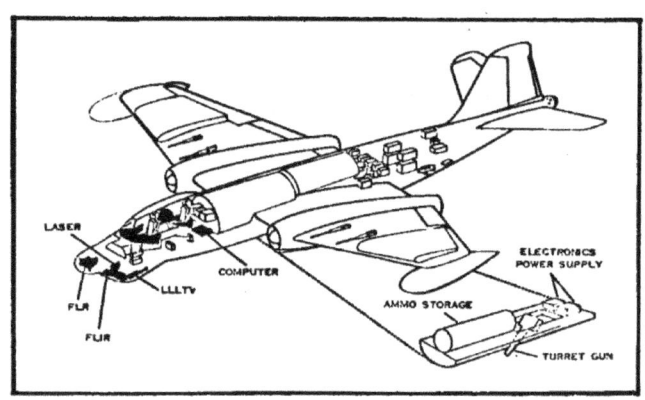

B-57G MODIFIED WITH PAVE GAT SYSTEM

Pave Gat personnel first had to decide whether the sensor slewed 20mm multi-barrel gun could be used in a B-57G. The Air Force amended Westinghouse's Tropic Moon II contract in December 1968 to include modification of the AN/AXQ-5 weapon delivery system to enable it to aim the gun. Emerson by early 1969 fabricated a gun turret to fit the B-57 bomb bay door. The Aeronautical Systems Division quickly carried out firing tests to prove that the turret worked, and Westinghouse reinstalled the modified AN/AXQ-5. Flight tests and live firing demonstrations followed, and by April 1970 the system had proven to be operationally and technically feasible.[10]/

Pave Gat's second task required testing a special 20mm armor piercing ammunition round. Made from extremely dense metal, the arrowhead-shaped flechette was designed to cause maximum damage to trucks and other vehicles. By the end of February 1970, the Armament Development and Test Center had demonstrated the ability of the Pave Gat weapon to fire the flechettes.[11]/

Westinghouse integrated the system into the B-57G in three phases--an engineering study, a prototype system, and a production plan. They subcontracted the engineering design study to Emerson, who by March 1970 determined the minor changes required to install the Pave Gat system in the B-57G. Westinghouse in April submitted a plan under which the Air Force would buy and test two prototype Pave Gat systems. Air Force headquarters optimistically asked that one prototype be tested at Eglin Air Force Base and the other at Ubon Royal Tahi Air Force Base during March 1971.

Because of the flexibility inherent in the rotary bomb bay door system of the B-57, Emerson was able to install two prototype turret systems on two doors without immobilizing a single aircraft. In October 1970, the Air Force delivered the B-57G that had been used for Category II tests to Westinghouse for Pave Gat modification. Westinghouse in November installed the first bomb bay door containing a Pave Gat turret. After flight tests in the Baltimore area, the Air Force flew the Pave Gat B-57G aircraft to Eglin Air Force Base in January 1971 and began testing. 12/

All had gone smoothly with Pave Gat because it was not in direct competition with other B-57G projects. When the Pave Gat B-57G reached Eglin, however, the single aircraft also was used in the radar remedial program, leading to a struggle over which program had priority. Pave Gat lost. The resultant delays in the Pave Gat tests forced the Air Staff to move the operational date from March to August, but even that proved overly optimistic. A spare parts shortage prevented mandatory aircraft maintenance; and during the 5 weeks beginning 9 April, the aircraft did not make a single Pave Gat flight. When Pave Gat missions resumed on 16 May, three of the first four scheduled missions were aborted because of aircraft equipment malfunctions, causing a loss of 3 more weeks. Those attending the B-57G program review meeting on 13 May 1971 deferred the Pave Gat operational date to October 1971. 13/

When Pave Gat tests finally proceeded they proved that the B-57G could hit stationary or moving targets with its 20mm gun, day or night. Loaded with 4,000 rounds of ammunition, the Pave Gat B-57G could hit as many as 20 targets, three times as many as the bomb-carrying B-57G. The Pave Gat aircraft could avoid antiaircraft fire by firing from offset positions, while the bomb carrier had to pass directly over the target. Categories II and III testing ended on 31 July 1971, and the Air Force looked forward to using the two Pave Gat prototype systems in the next interdiction campaign.14/

Because the Air Force had decided in August 1971 to return the B-57G squadron to the United States early in 1972, the Seventh and Thirteenth Air Forces, joined others in opposing combat testing of Pave Gat. The Air Force Systems Command calculated that sending the single Pave Gat prototype aircraft to Ubon would cost $500,000; installing the second prototype turret system in a B-57G already at Ubon would cost $350,000; and shipping both prototype turret systems to Southeast Asia and installing them would cost $950,000. Tactical Air Command also opposed flying the Pave Gat prototype to Southeast Asia because of seasonal adverse weather along the deployment route. Lt. Gen. George J. Eade, Deputy Chief of Staff for Plans and Operations at Air Force headquarters, opposed sending either the Pave Gat aircraft or the turrets because the system could be operational for less than 90 days, hardly enough time for a valid test.15/

While awaiting a decision from Air Force headquarters, Westinghouse removed the special test instrumentation from the Pave Gat prototype. A decision on 21 December 1971 terminated Project Pave Gat. Three and a half years of development and an expenditure of more than $4 million had failed to produce a single minute of combat time. Pave Gat had demonstrated, however, that sensor slewed guns could function effectively in a jet bomber.16/

Video Recorder

Because the Air Staff viewed the B-57G as an interim weapon system, a step on the way to the ultimate self-contained night attack aircraft, it sought a means of "acquainting senior officers and civilians with the capabilities of the system." The Tactical Air Warfare Center recommended that the Air Force equip the B-57G to record and assess its own strike damage. In response, the Air Staff established a requirement for recording the B-57G's low light level television presentation, an approach that had been used to evaluate the results of strikes by the AC-130 gunships. The video tapes would provide a first hand feel for the B-57G's night performance.

(C) On 2 March 1971, Air Force headquarters told Systems Command and PACAF to have two operational video tape recorders in use in Southeast Asia by 15 April. Systems Command on 8 March asked the Aeronautical Systems Division to give the project a "quick look" without interfering with the radar remedial program, and within a week the Systems Division had conceived a plan. For $81,000, Westinghouse agreed to buy two video recorder systems from Ball Brothers and then install both systems in B-57Gs in Southeast Asia. Air Force headquarters on 31 March allocated the necessary funds from Project 1559, which was normally used for Southeast Asia aircraft modification. [17]/

Cost overruns began almost at once. Westinghouse in April further studied the Ball Brothers' system and evaluated a similar system made by General Instruments. The Aeronautical Systems Division asked for an additional $35,000 for this Westinghouse "engineering evaluation," another $29,000 for "update required for limited qualification of the selected recorder," and $7,500 for three projectors. The Systems Division also learned that modification of all of the B-57Gs to carry the recorders would cost an additional $172,000. The Air Force Systems Command forwarded only the request for the additional $35,000 to Air Force headquarters, which on 13 May told the Systems Division not to contract for the entire program, and pointedly asked for an "austere and temporary" project to install video tape recorders in two B-57G aircraft for 6 months.[18]

The video tape recorder project was next slowed by equipment problems. The system tested at MacDill Air Force Base performed so poorly that the Air Force Armament Laboratory returned it to the factory in July 1971. It was September before the Aeronautical Systems Division was able to flight-test the recorders, and by then personnel of the B-57G squadron were clamoring for their delivery to Southeast Asia. A factory trained engineer reached Ubon Air Force Base in November with the recorders, and by 29 November he had them installed.[19]

Technically operational, the video tape recorder system had a major flaw that rendered it virtually useless. The B-57Gs bombs landed behind the aircraft, but the electro-optical sensors could not look back. Consequently the recorder was useless unless the B-57G maneuvered for a postattack pass, but all agreed that such a tactic was not "successful or feasible in a combat environment."

Further, Westinghouse had modified the low light level television system to shut down just before bomb impact so the flash from the explosion would not damage the TV tube. As that shutdown occurred, the recorder had to shift to the forward looking infrared sensor, but unless the two were closely synchronized, the infrared sensor would not record the bomb impact. Systems Command proposed dropping the project because of the almost insurmountable problems, but Air Force headquarters on 17 February 1972 insisted that the problem be found and corrected. Systems Command replied on 3 March that it was not very hopeful about the possibilities for a fix, and the following day the 8th Tactical Fighter Wing notified the Thirteenth Air Force that the Westinghouse engineer at Ubon was having no success. Only a month remained before the scheduled redeployment of the 13th Bombardment Squadron so Air Force headquarters finally halted the project.[20/] Months before, the attempt to improve the B-57G's navigation had met a similar fate.

Long-Range Navigation (LORAN)

Probably the best navigation method in use in Southeast Asia was LORAN D, a system precise enough to guide bombing missions. With LORAN equipment, B-57G crews could determine positions and plot courses to new target areas with speed and accuracy, and a LORAN-equipped B-57G could call LORAN target coordinates to similarly equipped fighters or gunships, or to airborne controllers or command centers. The Seventh Air Force used both arguments in July 1970 in Required Operational Capability 54-70 which called for installing the LORAN systems in all B-57Gs at Ubon RTAFB. PACAF at first indicated approval of the idea, but in August asked the Seventh Air Force for detailed information concerning the existing B-57G navigation system, the expected improvement resulting from installation of LORAN and the cost involved.[21]/

The Air Staff calculated a 16-month lead time for equipment installation, and there were already too few LORAN sets for the strike aircraft in Southeast Asia. Plans called for a reduction of the B-57G forces to six aircraft in the spring of 1972 and to none a year later. The navigation system already installed in the B-57G was adequate for the evaluation program and as accurate as any other set in aircraft not equipped with LORAN. By November 1970, the Seventh Air Force, PACAF, and Air Force headquarters had agreed to cancel ROC 54-70 and to terminate all consideration of a LORAN system for the B-57G. In March 1971, the Seventh Air Force advised the 8th Tactical Fighter Wing at Ubon of the cancellation.[22]/

Other Improvement Efforts

Texas Instruments in February 1971 asked for $99,500 to modify one of the forward looking infrared sensors to increase its range, improve the display quality, and reduce maintenance time. Improving all of the infrared sensors would cost $2.3 million. The Aeronautical Systems Division studied the offer in July and declined it. Air Force headquarters directed that favorable consideration be given only to changes that remedied an operational defect.[23]/

Although the B-57G specifications assumed a full hour of loiter time in the target area, the operational aircraft were much heavier than expected, and loiter time was shortened by several minutes. It would have been possible to increase the time over the target with in-flight refueling, but the Air Force Systems Command in 1970 estimated that installation of the refueling equipment would cost $845,000 and consume 1,700 man-hours, a prohibitively expensive project. Systems Command resurrected the idea in May 1971, but by then the Air Force no longer was interested in additional B-57G capability.24/

Gen. Lucius D. Clay, Seventh Air Force commander, wanted to lighten the B-57Gs by removing the unused 600-pound AN/ALT-28 jammers, but Headquarters, 7/13th Air Force and 8th Tactical Fighter Wing objected. Removal of the jammers would actually save only 100 pounds, because they would have to be replaced by 500 pounds of lead ballast to keep the aircraft in balance. In support of retaining the jammers, the 8th Tactical Fighter Wing observed that ". . . operations (personnel) feel much more at ease in knowing that they have a countermeasure capability they can employ against such (radar or surface-to-air missile) threats." The jammers remained in the aircraft.25/ Sensor development and modification practically came to a halt, but squadron operations, begun more than 2 years earlier, continued.

CHAPTER V -- COMBAT OPERATIONS

(U) Only two squadrons of B-57s remained in the Air Force active inventory by the mid-1960s--the 8th and 13th Bombardment Squadrons, Tactical, at Clark Air Base. Both squadrons maintained temporary duty detachments at Bien Hoa or Da Nang Air Bases from which their B-57Bs attacked targets in South Vietnam, Laos and the lower panhandle of North Vietnam. Combat attrition, accidents, and old age took their toll of the aircraft, and the withdrawal of B-57Bs for modification to the B-57G self-contained night attack configuration further reduced the number of available B-57s. PACAF inactivated the 13th Bombardment Squadron on 15 January 1968.

The 13th Bombardment Squadron, Tactical

(U) To provide a squadron to take the B-57G aircraft to Southeast Asia, TAC on 23 January 1969 reactivated the 13th Bomber Squadron,

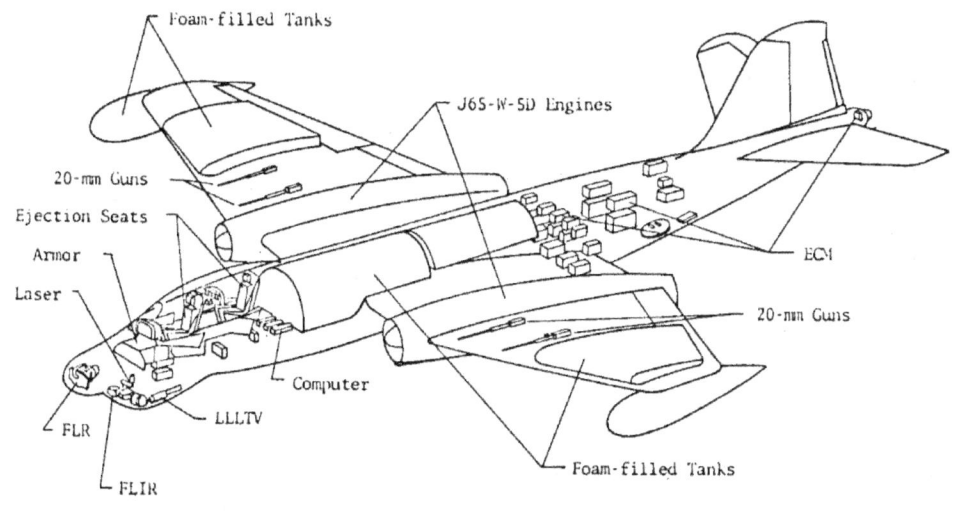

SECRET **B-57G CONFIGURATION**

Tactical, at MacDill AFB, Florida, and assigned it to the 15th Tactical Fighter Wing. The newly reactivated unit had planned to fly to Southeast Asia in December 1969 to use the new sensors against enemy truck convoys during the dry season in Laos, and to develop the necessary tactics and techniques and evaluate the sensors and special equipment. By the end of June 1969, the 13th Squadron had 29 officers and 135 airmen, but not a single aircraft. The extended waiting period could have been disastrous to the morale of the personnel, but the 15th Tactical Fighter Wing and higher echelons took advantage of the lull to increase the proficiency of both flying and nonflying personnel. During July and August, the squadron sent selected flying crews and aircraft maintenance personnel to the Westinghouse Technical Training Center at Baltimore, Maryland, for special factory training in the use and maintenance of the new equipment. Aircraft maintenance personnel also attended special training courses at Hill Air Force Base and later worked on the B-57s of the 4424th Combat Crew Training Squadron. In addition to receiving basic B-57B training with the 4424th at MacDill Air Force Base, the flying crews attended basic survival school at Fairchild Air Force Base, water survival school at Homestead Air Force Base, and air-ground operations school at Eglin Air Force Base. A Link simulator for the B-57G arrived at MacDill Air Force Base in mid-December to provide an additional training device for the flying personnel.1/

(U) Until the B-57Gs arrived, the pilots and navigators needed every bit of training help they could get. They flew in the B-57s of the 4424th Training Squadron as often as possible, but the 4424th's heavy training schedule limited such flights. Some navigators managed to log flying time in the base's C-47 aircraft, but that hardly contributed to their flying proficiency. Trying to accumulate the flying time required by Air Force Manual 60-1, many pilots and navigators went on cross-country flights at their own expense, there being no temporary duty finds available. Work on the base runway between 30 July and 24 September closed the field to flying for 4 days each week, a further impediment. Before the end of the year, the Air Force added three B-57E aircraft to the 4424th Combat Crew Training Squadron's inventory and earmarked them for proficiency flying by the 13th Bombardment Squadron. The Air Force provided no additional maintenance or support personnel to care for the added aircraft, so it was fortunate that the 4424th could borrow such personnel from the 13th. By the end of the year, the 13th Bombardment Squadron had 13 pilots and 20 navigators fully qualified in the B-57C, and was flying three sorties per day with B-57Es.[2/]

Delayed delivery of the modified aircraft had forced the Air Force to slip the departure date to June 1970, but the growing number of problems began to make even that date seem more improbable. Air Force headquarters on 11 March 1970 announced that the 13th Bombardment Squadron would go to Southeast Asia on 15 September 1970, a further slippage of 3 months. The squadron took delivery of its first B-57G on 26 May and received three more before the end of the month, but the continuing problems and the substantial unfulfilled training requirements again made the departure date appear unrealistic.

When representatives of Air Force headquarters, Air Force Systems Command, and Tactical Air Command met on 9 July 1970 to discuss the 13th Bombardment Squadron, they agreed that it was highly unlikely that the squadron could be combat-ready by

15 September. General Ferguson, Systems Command commander, and General Momyer, Tactical Air commander, agreed and said they would rather delay the departure a full year than send a squadron to Southeast Asia with an aircraft weapon system that was not combat-ready. They formally recommended that the Air Force Chief of Staff slip the 13th Bombardment Squadron's departure date to 15 October 1970. Should the squadron not be able to meet even that date, they proposed delaying until the 1971-72 Laos dry season. General Ryan, Air Force Chief of Staff, terming such a delay "inconsistent with the total improvement we are endeavoring to get into Southeast Asia for the next interdiction campaign," directed the formation of an Air Staff team to proceed at once to MacDill Air Force Base to review the program and take whatever remedial action was necessary. The team, headed by Brig. Gen. Carroll H. Bolender, was composed of key Air Staff personnel from operations, development, the inspector general, supply, and maintenance engineering.3/

Moreover matters beyond Air Force control threatened further delays and problems. A noncommissioned officer of the 13th Squadron complained to his congressman that his unit was "unprepared" for the pending move to Southeast Asia because the aircraft were not ready. The General Accounting Office investigated and announced that readiness was a judgment decision that only the U.S. Air Force could make.4/

Meanwhile, a tricommand committee came into being to solve the B-57G problems. Systems, Tactical Air, and Logistics Commands each contributed a team, led by a colonel, to meet at MacDill Air Force Base weekly to investigate current problems, assign action items for accomplishment by the appropriate team, and monitor

B-57G CONTRACT PROGRESS

Sequence	A/C Serial	To Westinghouse	AF Acceptance	Remarks
1	53-3928	9 Aug 68	2 Mar 70	Cat I Test
2	53-3905	12 Aug 68	None	Crashed, 16 Dec 69
3	53-3906	12 Aug 68	None	Cat II, Pave Gat, Radar remedial
4	53-3931	13 Dec 68	23 May 70	
5	53-3886	16 Dec 68	13 Apr 70	Cat III Test
6	53-3889	17 Dec 68	8 Apr 70	Cat III Test
7	53-3929	13 Jan 69	29 Apr 70	Cat III Test
8	53-3865	15 Jan 69	26 Feb 70	Munitions cert.
9	52-1588	15 Jan 69	28 May 70	
10	52-1582	15 Jan 69	29 May 70	
11	52-1578	22 Jan 69	20 Jun 70	(Date disputed)
12	53-3877	9 Apr 69	29 May 70	
13	53-3898	14 Apr 69	20 Jun 70	
14	53-3860	24 Apr 69	6 Aug 70	
15	52-1580	30 Apr 69	4 Aug 70	
16	53-3878	19 May 69	27 Aug 70	

progress on corrective actions. Tactical Air Command also told the committee to refer matters beyond its competence to the commanders of TAC or Systems Command. The appropriate command then could initiate action to preclude further adverse impact on the B-57G departure date. The committee met through the summer of 1970 and effectively solved several major problems before disbanding early in September.5/

With committees and teams proliferating, Air Force Systems Command on 10 August called for a general officer review of the B-57G program on 13 August. As a result, the commanders of Tactical Air, Systems, and Logistics Commands recommended that eleven B-57Gs leave on 15 September as scheduled.6/ The Chief of Staff approved that recommendation.

To ready its B-57Gs for the flight to Thailand, the squadron stopped all flying in the United States by 4 September. On 24 August, Gen. John C. Meyer, Vice Chief of Staff, asked that the general officers reconvene on 1 September for a final evaluation of the decision to transfer the B-57Gs on 15 September. The group found that the squadron had made slow but gradual progress toward readiness, but had not completed its training requirements. Nevertheless, the general officers again recommended a 15 September 1970 departure.[7]/

Having completed most of the required training, the squadron began final preparations to leave. To allow the aircraft to carry as large a fuel load as possible, the manufacturer, as noted earlier, removed all nonessential sensors and equipment and shipped them to Southeast Asia as air freight. The movement plan divided the aircraft into three flights of three, and one flight of two aircraft. The carefully planned route took the aircraft north to Elmendorf Air Force Base, Alaska, thence to Adak, Midway, Wake, Guam, Okinawa, and the Philippines. Under average wind conditions at the worst time of the year, the leg from Adak to Midway left the aircraft with only about a 30-minute fuel reserve, making good weather forecasting particularly important. Each crew and aircraft flew at least two cruise-control missions just before leaving to insure that the ferry tanks worked and that the crews could accomplish the precision flying and navigation needed for the long overwater flights.

Under TAC/USAFSTRIKE Operations Plan 100, the Air Force in July 1970 ordered the 13th Bombardment Squadron to Thailand in a movement nicknamed Coronet Condor. With the orders confirmed, an airlift control element team of one officer and four enlisted men flew to Ubon Royal Thai Air Force Base to provide control and support for the transport aircraft that would carry the squadron maintenance personnel and equipment. General Meyer on 14 September sent word to the squadron that he, General Ryan, and Air Force Secretary Seamans fully supported the new concept and would be watching the squadron in its evaluation of the new equipment and techniques. He quoted Secretary Seamans as saying that the B-57Gs were the vanguard of the future night attack system, providing the baseline for evaluating new systems in the years ahead. With that farewell message, the Air Force sent the 13th Bombardment Squadron, Tactical, to combat.8/

The Deployment

(U) With little fanfare, the B-57Gs flew from MacDill Air Force Base to Tinker Air Force Base on 15 September 1970, a short first leg to allow the crews and aircraft to ease into the longer days ahead. Thunderstorms the next morning delayed the takeoff, forcing the squadron to remain overnight at Mountain Home Air Force Base rather than continuing on into Canada as scheduled. The crews made up lost time the next day, however, by refueling at Comox

Airfield, Canada, and flying on to Elmendorf AFB, Alaska. All aircraft arrived without incident.

(U) Because Adak could handle only half of the squadron at a time, two flights of three aircraft each flew to that Aleutian base while the five other aircraft remained at Elmendorf Air Force Base. Headwinds along the route to Midway caused a 1-day delay, but five of the aircraft from Adak made the flight to Midway on 20 September.

B-57G DEPLOYMENT ROUTE

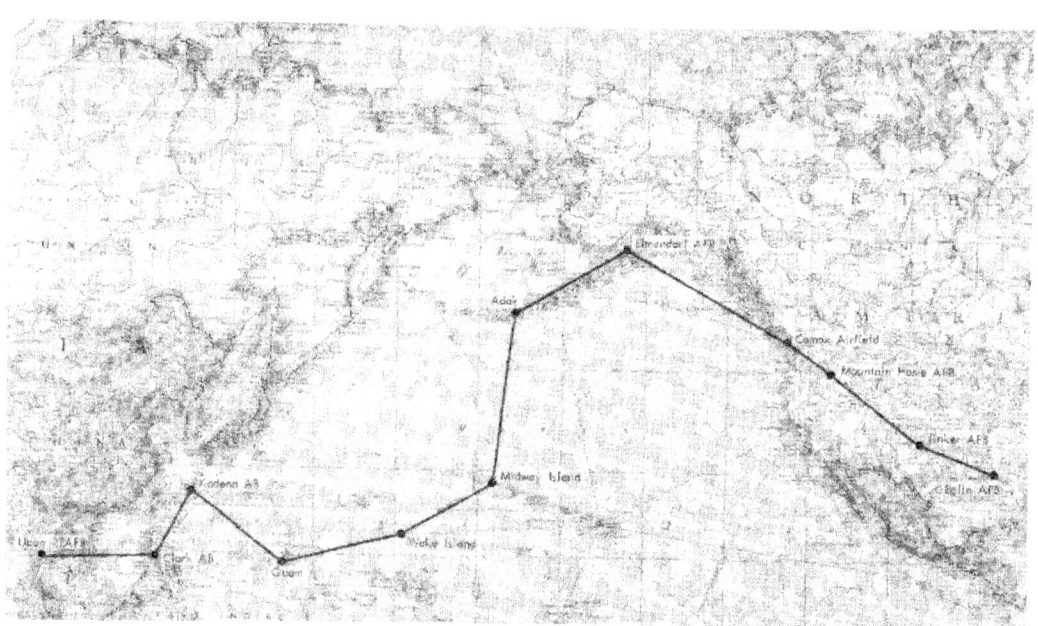

Four of the five B-57Gs at Elmendorf Air Force Base moved to Adak that day, leaving behind one aircraft with an oxygen system problem. One of the three maintenance teams accompanying the flight in C-130 aircraft repaired a minor engine problem in a B-57G at Adak and another worked on the defective oxygen system at Elmendorf Air Force Base. Nine of the B-57Gs hopped on into Wake and Guam, where they spend 3 days waiting for the two B-57Gs with maintenance problems to catch up.

(U) Three flights of three aircraft took off from Guam on 28 September to fly to Kadena Air Base, but one aircraft in the third cell turned back with a leaking tip tank. The eight B-57Gs spent the night on Okinawa, and the next day seven of them flew to Clark Air Base, refueled, and landed at Ubon that afternoon. The one aircraft left at Kadena Air Base for maintenance work was joined on 29 September by the three aircraft from Guam. All four flew to Clark Air Base the next morning and reached Ubon by evening.

In addition to the three C-130's carrying the enroute support teams, twelve C-141 aircraft carried the squadron equipment and personnel and a reinstallation team of Aeronautical Systems Division and Texas Instrument technicians. The first C-141 arrived at Ubon on 16 September, and the others followed in a carefully planned sequence. During the first 12 days of October, the reinstallation team unpacked and reinstalled the sensors and other equipment to prepare the B-57Gs for combat. Meanwhile, the crews attended orientation briefings on rules of engagement and local flying procedures. All flying personnel ultimately attended the Pacific Air Forces' jungle survival school, and Task Force Alpha personnel at Nakhom Phanom Royal Thai Air Force Base briefed them on the sensors, computers, and other components of the electronic infiltration barrier. Before it could be classified combat ready, each crew had to complete one local flight over Thailand, one high altitude daylight flight with F-4D escort over a reasonably safe portion of Laos, and six unescorted combat sorties in relatively low threat areas of Laos. As soon as they became combat-ready, the crews began flying scheduled night sorties over the eastern portion of the Laos panhandle.9/

Commando Hunt V

With almost clockwork precision, the monsoon wind shift each October brought cool northeast breezes to Laos, drying the muddy roads and clearing away the clouds. North Vietnam sent its trucks pouring southward through the panhandle of Laos, and the United States simultaneously increased its aerial strikes against both the roads and the trucks. Beginning with the Laos dry season of 1968-69, the Air Force nicknamed the interdiction campaigns Commando Hunt. The Air Force estimated that Commando Hunt I destroyed or damaged 6,000 trucks and permitted only about 20 percent of the supplies entering Laos to reach South Vietnam. During the 1969-70 dry season, Commando Hunt had destroyed an estimated 20,000 trucks and allowed approximately one-third of the supplies to reach South Vietnam. Following the deposition of Prince Norodom Sihanouk, Cambodia closed its seaport of Kompong Som to the North Vietnamese, leading U.S. planners to expect an even heavier flow of trucks and supplies through eastern Laos during the 1970-71 dry

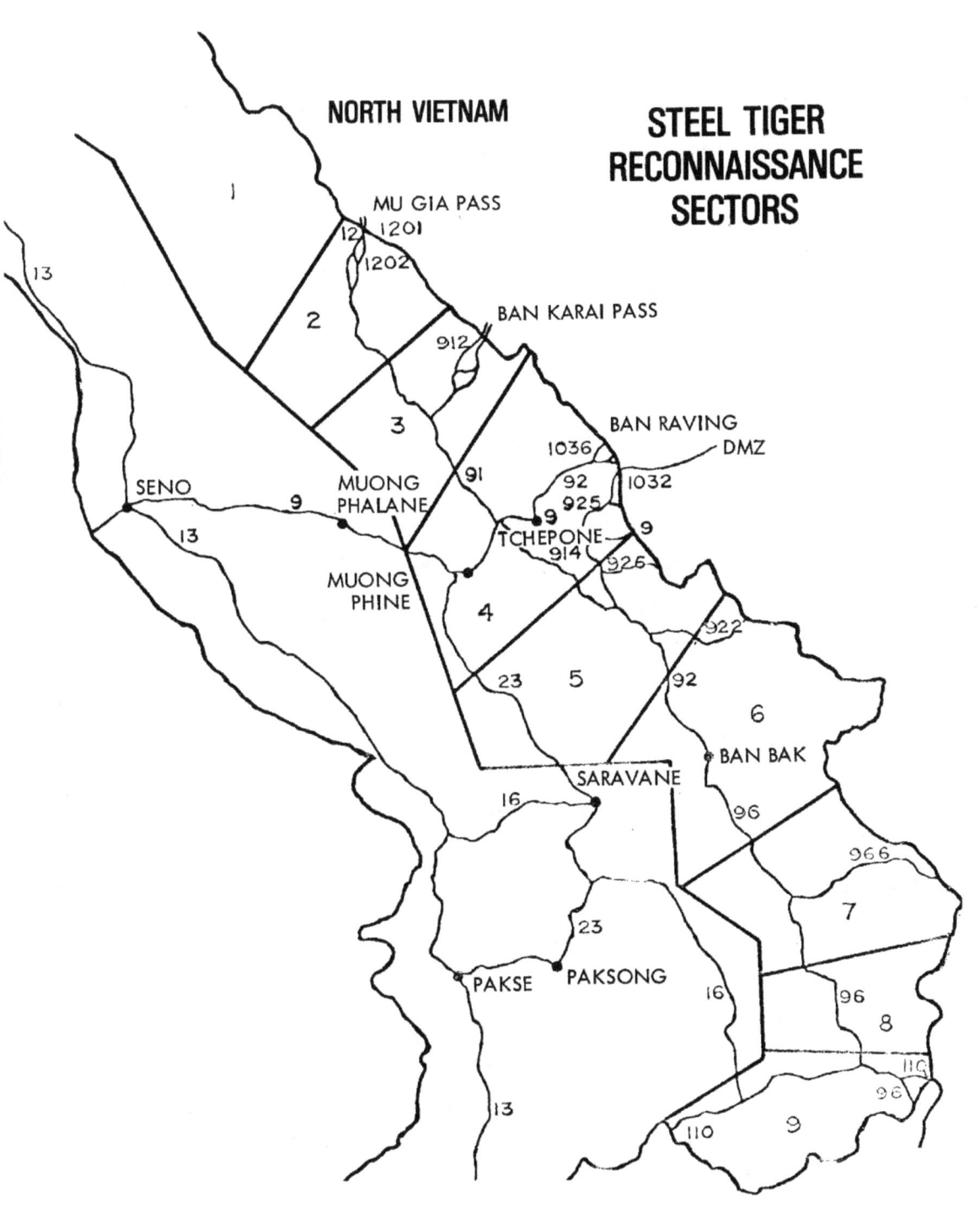

season. Commando Hunt V planned to restrict that flow with a force of fighters augmented by an enlarged gunship force and the eleven B-57Gs. 10/

Many of the B-57G maintenance problems, discussed earlier, had not been solved prior to the flight to Thailand, and they continued to plague the squadron at Ubon. Tactical Air Command had arranged for a team of civilian contractor specialists to remain at Ubon, and Pacific Air Forces was expected to modify the size and composition of the team as the squadron gained experience with the B-57G maintenance needs. 11/

While the maintenance function worked itself into shape, the squadron began combat missions in Commando Hunt V. This activity called for searches along roads and waterways at night to detect, recognize, and destroy or assist in destroying targets normally concealed by the night. The squadron flew its first armed combat mission on the night of 17/18 October 1970, but low clouds obscured the ground in the target area and all of the B-57Gs brought their bombs back to base. Flights continued, but it was a week later before a B-57G destroyed the first truck credited to the 13th Bombardment Squadron. 12/

From this point on, the B-57G lost little time in proving its ability to kill trucks. This was brought out in the report of a special team which evaluated the 13th Squadron during the first 3 months of combat (17 October 1970-15 January 1971). On 543 sorties, the B-57G crews sighted 759 trucks, attacked 565, and destroyed 363. Although this 0.67 trucks destroyed per sortie fell below the predicted 6.9 kill per sortie ratio, the statistics included many sorties on which no trucks were seen. Unusually poor weather through the end of November 1970 kept the number of trucks moving through Laos at a surprisingly low level. When targets were available, the B-57G could find and destroy them despite a number of handicaps.13/

The squadron flew all of its missions in the eastern part of the so-called Steel Tiger area of Laos which extended along the borders of North and South Vietnam from the Cambodian border to north of the Mu Gia Pass. The Seventh Air Force had divided Steel Tiger East into 14 visual reconnaissance areas, designated VR-1 through VR-14, and scheduled the B-57Gs into specific VR areas on each mission. While large numbers of trucks moved through Laos during this period, they were not evenly distributed but often were concentrated along certain roads. The B-57G could remain in the area less than an hour and carried a maximum of six bombs, while the gunships (against which they were compared) could hunt trucks for up to 4 hours and carried enough ammunition to attack several targets. Because the AC-130 and AC-119 gunships reported spectacular results, the Seventh Air Force scheduled them into the more lucrative target areas and used the B-57Gs to fill gaps in gunship coverage and to cover visual reconnaissance areas where fewer trucks could be expected. Consequently, the B-57Gs encountered a scarcity of targets, particularly early in the evaluation period when the truck flow was a mere trickle.14/

Despite a number of equipment problems and the scarcity of targets, the kill statistics gradually improved until by the end of Commando Hunt V, the B-57Gs in 1,202 sorties had attacked 2,841 trucks and damaged or destroyed 1,931. Again, this 1.6 truck per sortie kill ratio fell below the 6.9 design goal, but the B-57Gs were establishing a record not too far behind that of the AC-130

STEEL TIGER EAST

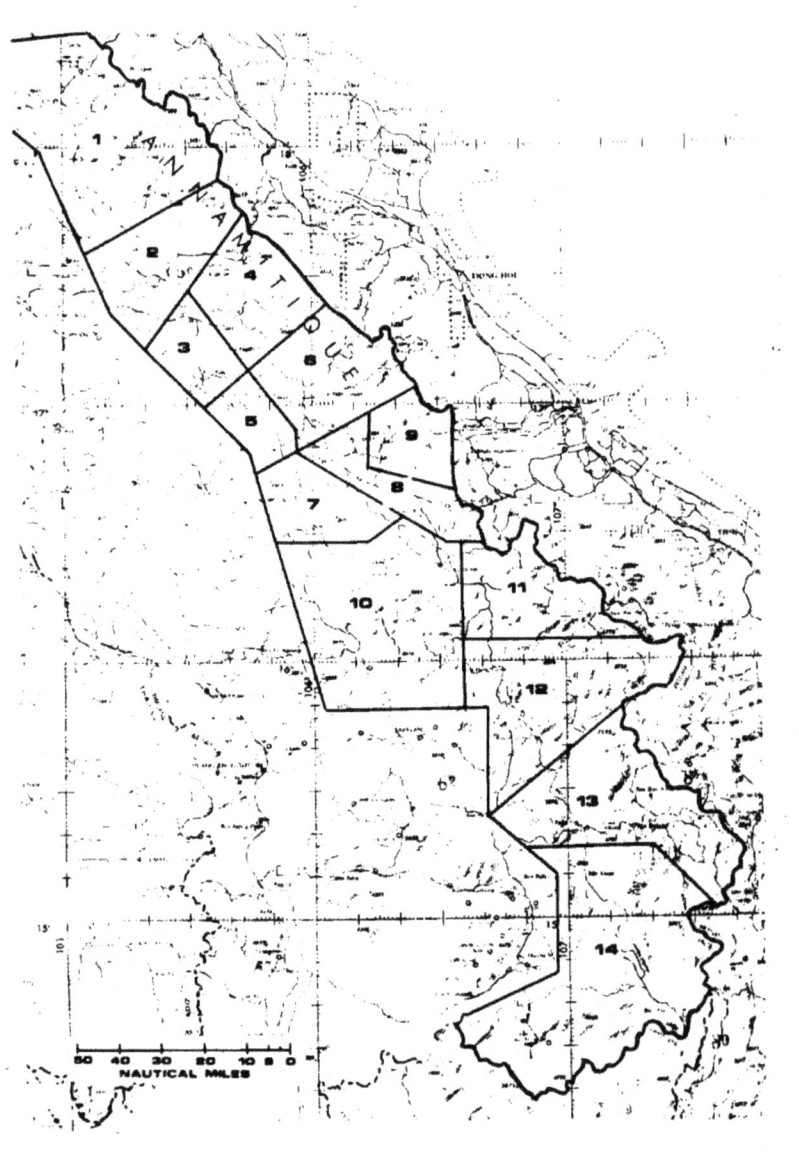

gunships and far better than the record of the fighter aircraft. While the yardstick for measuring effectiveness was destruction of trucks, the 13th Bombardment Squadron also destroyed a ferry, a boat, and had caused at least 280 secondary explosions and 255 fires. 15/

Combat tactics evolved as the crews became more familiar with the equipment and the flying conditions in eastern Laos. After takeoff, the B-57G pilot climbed to high altitude for the trip to the search area, and descended to operating altitude only after a radio coordination with other aircraft in the area and clearance from the area controller. The pilot normally flew at 250 knots true airspeed at 6,000 feet above ground level while searching for and identifying targets, although the altitude frequently was increased to 8,000 feet whenever there was more than a quarter moon. The sensor operator activated the computer to steer the aircraft to the target, altering headings as needed to maintain the desired field of view with the active sensor. All of the sensors fed data to the computer to keep it updated, but until computer reliability improved and the operators became more familiar with the area, it was necessary for the sensor operator to make frequent cross checks with the TACAN/DME (distance measuring equipment) set. 16/

As soon as the sensor operator identified a target, he switched to "track" and gave the pilot steering information for a straight and level weapon delivery. Most often, however, identification came too late for a first-pass attack, forcing the pilot to make a second pass. The computer remembered the target position and the pilot could elect to have the computer return the aircraft to the target on any one of several different flight patterns. The computer continued to present steering information to the pilot throughout the attack, and could release the weapons automatically.[17]

On the first missions, the B-57Gs carried only three types of weapons--the M-36 fire bomb, the Mk-82 laser-guided bomb, and the Hayes PW4/4A modular bomb dispenser. Normal bomb loads were four M-36s carried internally with two Mk-82s on the wing pylons, or a Hayes dispenser with 22 canisters of BLU-26 bomblets. When the air temperature at Ubon became too high for a safe takeoff with a full bomb load, the squadron reduced the internal bomb load by one or two bombs. Released at 6,000 feet above ground level, the M-36 firebomb canisters opened at 1,500 feet, giving a satisfactory dispersion of the bomblets. Over high threat areas a higher release altitude was more desirable for both aircraft safety and bomblet dispersal, but the altitude was limited by the sensors and the available light. The crew released the Mk-82 ballistically and guided it to the target with the B-57G laser ranger-illuminator.[18]

Enemy antiaircraft defenses quickly developed tactics to counter the night flying bombers. The crews found it desirable to avoid preplanned ("canned") headings and altitudes when entering the search areas because the enemy massed antiaircraft weapons along such routes. B-57G pilots frequently became engrossed in killing a truck and made several passes, even though they knew such a procedure to be highly dangerous. Quite frequently they found that by the third or fourth pass, they were turning into antiaircraft fire that had not been there earlier. Enemy gunners often held their fire until the B-57G dropped a bomb in their vicinity at which time they opened up. Some pilots also reported that enemy gunners at times seemed to be firing at random, possibly at the

B-57G WITH TWO EXTERNAL MK-82 LASER GUIDED BOMBS
AND FOUR M-36E2S IN INTERNAL BOMB BAY

B-57 EXTERNAL CARRIAGE
OF MK-82 LASER GUIDED
BOMB (500 POUNDS)

M-36 INCENDIARY BOMB

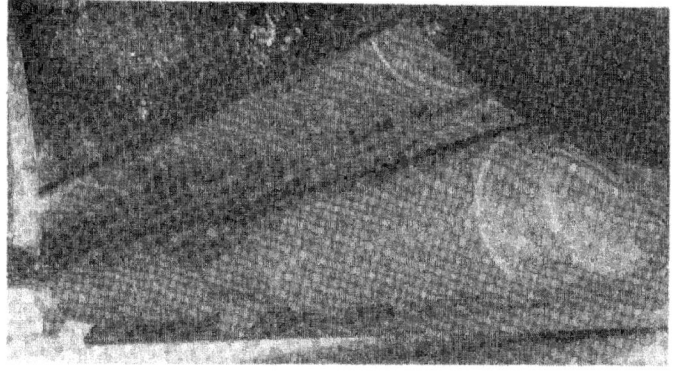

aircraft sound.[19] In any event, the growing enemy antiaircraft defenses constituted a serious threat to the night attack aircraft.

Exactly how serious a threat existed was forcibly demonstrated to the 13th Bombardment Squadron on 12 December 1970. The squadron commander, Lt. Col. Paul R. Pitt, and Lt. Col. Edwin A. Buschette, senior sensor operator, took off from Ubon to fly a search mission in the Steel Tiger area between Tchepone and the South Vietnam border. The crew destroyed one truck with an M-36 fire bomb and moved to another area to search for more moving trucks. A forward air controller vectored the B-57G to moving trucks along Route 9, but clouds obscured the target on the first two passes. Just before weapon release on the third pass, something struck the aircraft and caused it to roll violently to the right. For a brief moment, Colonel Pitt thought he might have collided with the O-2 forward air controller aircraft, but Colonel Buschette was certain that the enemy antiaircraft defenses had made a lucky hit. With the aircraft out of control, the crew ejected and landed without injury. Both downed airmen used their survival radios to make voice contact with rescue aircraft and made plans for a dawn pickup. Colonel Buschette was concerned when dawn showed that he had chosed an unoccupied enemy shelter for his hiding place, but he neither saw nor heard enemy troops. Bad weather was forecast in the area that morning, but shortly after dawn the skies unexpectedly cleared so the helicopter could pick up both crew members and return them to Thailand. Fighter aircraft destroyed the B-57G wreckage with napalm to keep the sensors from falling into enemy hands.[20]

Maintenance problems had caused the temporary loss of another B-57G a few days earlier. One aircraft had turned back during six missions because of indications of engine overhead conditions or fire warnings. On a 3 December 1970 mission the pilot, Maj. William O. Rothlisberger, already had aborted his mission because of a malfunctioning computer and was on his way back to Ubon when the fire warning light came on once more. The pilot landed the aircraft with a fire in the wing and a smoke-filled cockpit. A broken clamp had allowed the tailpipe of number one engine to separate from the tail cone and flame from the engine set fire to the wing, damaging it beyond local repair. When a replacement B-57E wing arrived from Davis-Monthan Air Force Base, factory engineers modified it to meet B-57G specifications and installed it. Until February 1971, however, the squadron had only nine B-57Gs operational.[21]

As the crews flew more operational missions, they began to isolate and define the equipment problems. Some involved highly technical equipment that could only be improved through better engineering and extensive modification, but many problems were as basic as cockpit lights that were too bright and could not be dimmed. To correct that particular problem, the pilots covered portions of each light with tape or grease pencil, crude but effective improvisations.[22]

Equipment Problems

In addition to the normal problems encountered by all squadrons, such as inadequate ramp space and a shortage of spare parts, the 13th Bombardment Squadron encountered unique maintenance problems with its highly specialized equipment. Failure rates for most of the electronic components far exceeded expectations, and there were not enough replacements. When the B-57Gs flew through rain, the radomes frequently filled with water, causing radar failure. The repair of major electronic components at U.S. factories took as long as 90 days, far too long in view of the short time between failures. The Military Airlift Command on 15 November 1970 moved its Thailand terminal from Khorat Royal Thai Air Force Base to Ubon, reducing the travel time to and from the United States for B-57G parts and components. By early 1971, the Air Force had reduced travel time for repaired components from 6 weeks to 10 days. The Warner-Robins Air Materiel Area also renegotiated the Texas Instruments contract to require that they repair radar components within 30 days rather than the original contract time of 90 days, and sent officers to each repair facility to expedite repair.[23]/

      Navigation accuracy was a major problem, both because of the type of equipment installed in the B-57Gs and the operational requirements established by the Seventh Air Force. B-57Gs scheduled into a particular visual reconnaissance area had to stay within the boundaries of that area for flying safety and to comply with the rules of engagement. To complicate the problem, many visual reconnaissance areas contained small "no-bomb" areas (mostly suspected or confirmed prisoner-of-war camps) which could not be bombed under any circumstances. At its cruising speed, a B-57G crossed the largest visual reconnaissance area in less than 20 minutes, and the smaller areas were only 2 or 3 minutes across. With navigation equipment designed to provide accuracy within 1 percent of the distance flown, the crew could find itself 1 to 2 miles off at a range of 125 nautical miles, enough to cause problems. Crews frequently abandoned targets which seemed too close to the no-bomb areas, fearing that the built-in error might cause their bombs to fall within those areas. Similarly, they cut short their patrol routes to avoid crossing into neighboring visual reconnaissance areas. Had the radar equipment worked properly, the crews could have confirmed their exact position, but they were denied that capability. Almost without exception, the crews recommended that future night attack aircraft have better self-contained navigation equipment.

Because it had been designed as a long-range target detector, the forward-looking radar was most important to the whole B-57G concept. Its failure thus contributed significantly to the reduced productivity of the entire system. Although the contractor made changes intended to correct the defects, it quickly became apparent that they had made no improvement. The moving target indicator feature remained totally inoperative, rendering the radar ineffective as a target locator. Early in 1971, an aircrew from the 13th Bombardment Squadron went to MacDill Air Force Base to evaluate contractor efforts, but they learned nothing of value.[24]

Beginning in June 1971, the squadron removed the forward looking radar sets from the aircraft and shipped them back to the Texas Instruments factory for modification. Eventually, all 10 aircraft were without radar sets. The first modified radar was returned to the squadron on 21 September and a joint Aeronautical Systems Division/Texas Instrument team began installation. A check flight on 27 September in aircraft number 582 indicated that the moving target indicator would work, but subsequent flights were less promising. All of the sets were reinstalled by November, and by the end of the month the moving target indicator had detected only three targets on 348 combat sorties. By early 1972, the evaluation had determined that the moving target indicator was not satisfactory for locating targets because of terrain clutter on the radar presentation, jungle canopies that concealed targets, and the excessive tuning time required. The moving target indicator never did function adequately, no matter how much effort went into it. (The terrain-following and terrain-avoidance features of the radar were neither needed nor evaluated.)[25/]

When the forward looking radar set failed to measure up to specifications, the shorter range low light level television and the forward looking infrared became the most important target acquisition sensors. Whenever there was sufficient moonlight, the television worked at longer ranges than expected, but it was ineffective during the dark of the moon. Throughout such periods, however, the forward looking infrared sensor was particularly valuable for detecting unlighted trucks at ranges up to 12,000 feet. But that was much too short a distance for a normal first-pass attack, forcing the B-57G crew either to abandon the target or to make a second pass to deliver its weapons. By early 1971 the TV picture tubes showed signs of deterioration, and spots appeared on the visual display. As long as the spots did not occur within the tracking gate--a rectangle near the center of the scope that looked at a ground area about 400 feet by 500 feet in size--the set remained usable. After acquiring targets for the laser-guided bombs, the operator switched the television to standby to prevent tube damage from the flash of the bomb burst, and the infrared sensor took over target tracking. Westinghouse engineers in July 1971 changed the program so the computer automatically switched off the TV set 4 seconds prior to estimated bomb impact, leaving the final tracking to the infrared sensor and the laser guidance system. The B-57G thus could deliver the Mk-82 laser-guided bombs only against targets that appeared on the display of its forward looking infrared sensor.[26]/

Although the forward looking infrared sensor worked well, it too had certain limitations. Its narrow field of view made target identification rather difficult; its range was limited by aircraft altitude and the density and temperature of the atmosphere; and it could not penetrate clouds or haze. It did have good image detection, however, and could be focused quickly and easily in flight.[27]/

Equally essential, the laser ranger-illuminator gave little trouble, but suffered from poor design. The laser equipment probably best illustrates the failure of the engineers to visualize the system in action. Inputs from the sensors permitted the computer to aim the laser ranger-illuminator at the target and to track it automatically. However, the ranger-illuminator could rotate only $4°$ to the rear, not far enough to keep a target illuminated until bomb impact when weapons release took place from level flight at 6,000 feet as required by the PACAF rules of engagement. The pilot therefore, had to maneuver the aircraft to keep the laser aimed at the target until the bombs detonated. The sensor operators quickly learned also that improper boresighting or careless tuning could cause the Mk-82 bombs to miss. Heavy haze could divert or reflect the laser energy, as could stray clouds moving across the target, thus causing the bombs to lose guidance and fall short. During the period April through June 1971, 306 Mk-82 bombs scored 215 direct hits, attesting to the accuracy of the system. Of the 73 that failed to guide, 8 were caused by crew error, 9 by weather, 18 by equipment malfunction, and 38 by unknown factors.[28/]

To correct at least some of the problems, a Westinghouse modification team at Ubon made a number of wiring changes in the B-57Gs between 15 July and 11 September 1971. They installed controls that allowed the pilot and sensor operator to vary the light intensity of the radar display tube, solving at least a part of the night vision problem. They also added a warning light to alert the pilot to inadequate air pressure in the radar waveguide, a source of many past radar malfunctions. Other wiring changes either corrected minor deficiencies or modified wiring networks to prevent particular problems from developing.[29/]

Only three sorties during the combat evaluation used the Hayes modular dispenser. On two of those sorties, the selected number of canisters failed to release, although there were no hung weapons as a result of that failure. Maintenance personnel found that rub strips were loose and warped, causing the rotary bomb bay door to jam; further use of the Hayes dispenser consequently was halted.

Even though the B-57G crews managed to deliver bombs successfully it was nevertheless difficult to assess the true bomb damage. The B-57G carried no cameras or other means of recording bomb impact, forcing evaluators to rely upon crew reports. In a few isolated cases, forward air controllers were able to determine and report bomb damage, but this was a haphazard process. Normal aerial reconnaissance missions the following morning did provide a small amount of bomb damage assessment, but they could not be depended upon for regular coverage of the B-57G strikes. And whenever the crews evaluated their own bomb damage, they subjected themselves to criticism for allegedly inflating the figures.

Equipment failures continued to plague the B-57G. Airframe and engine spare parts, initially scarce, eventually became available in sufficient quantity to keep the operationally ready rate at an acceptable level. The squadron, however, never had sufficient spare parts available to keep navigation equipment, computer, and sensor functioning. Although the maintenance situation improved gradually, the B-57G needed more than 56 maintenance man-hours for every hour of flying time.

The Rainy Season

During the rainy season in Laos in April and May, the roads generally were impassable to the North Vietnamese truck convoys and the B-57Gs had few targets. The Commando Hunt VI interdiction campaign began in the lower panhandle of North Vietnam, but the B-57Gs were limited to Laos for combat missions and did not participate in the new program. New pilots and sensor operators began arriving, and the reduced combat mission tempo provided sufficient aircraft to permit speedy indoctrination of the new crews. As the squadron removed the forward looking radar sets from the B-57Gs, it gradually reduced the number of aircraft it could fly over Laos, until by the end of August not a single B-57G was available for these missions. 30/

To overcome its lack of radar sets and the restrictions imposed by weather, the squadron established a closer working relationship with Task Force Alpha, the unit that operated the

ROAD NETWORK, CENTRAL LAOS

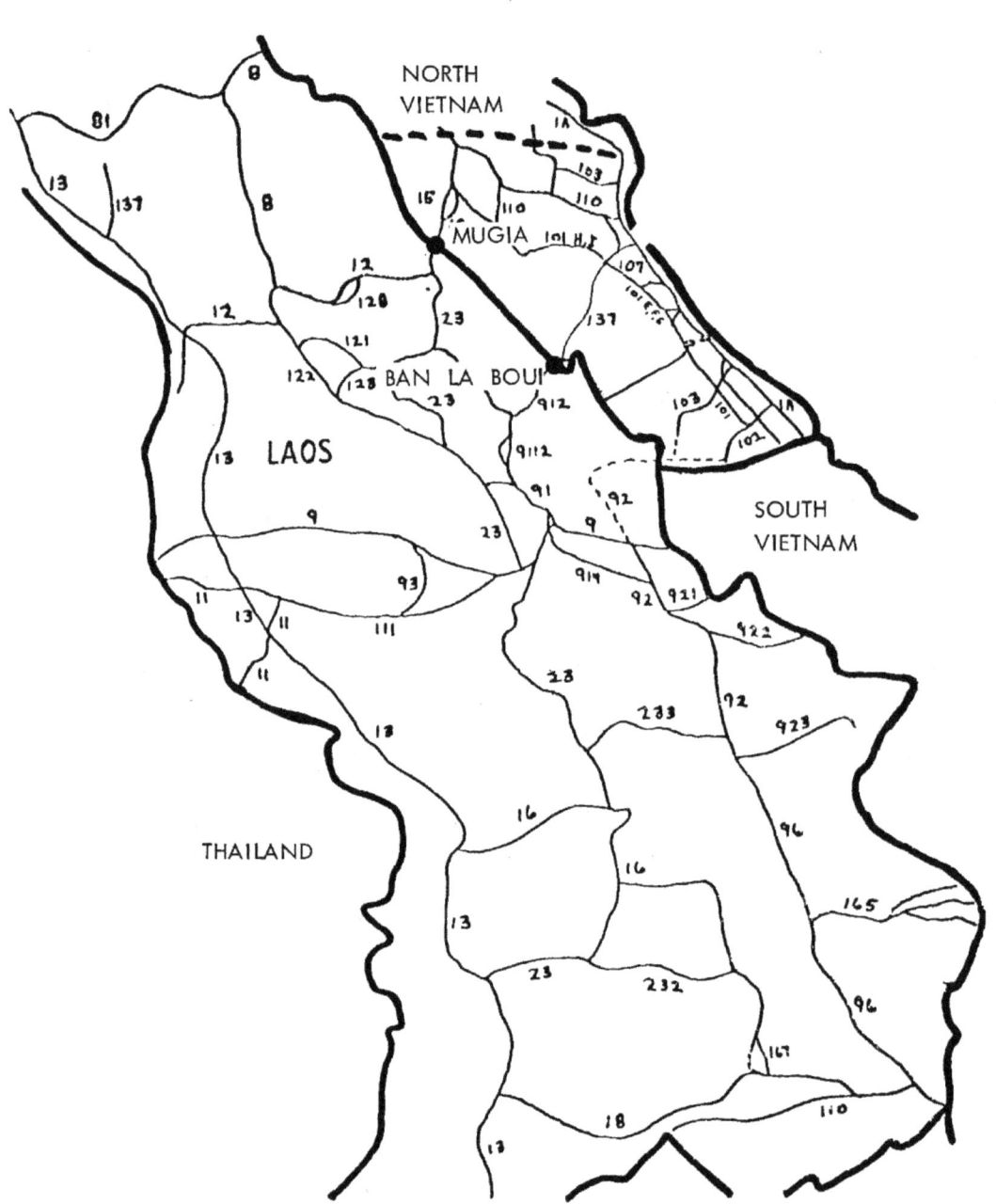

electronic infiltration barrier in Laos. Whenever the Task Force Alpha sensors pinpointed moving trucks in the B-57G area, the task force passed the information to the crew by secure voice radio. If Task Force Alpha provided coordinates, the crew could insert them into the computer and automatically fly directly to the spot, but if only a TACAN bearing and distance was provided, the pilot had to maneuver to that position. Meanwhile, the sensor operator prepared for the attack. Once the aircraft acquired the target on its own sensors, it went ahead with a normal bombing mission.31/

When not receiving target data from Task Force Alpha, the B-57Gs flew routine search missions, principally along Route 23 in central Laos. But this was not enough to keep the aircraft busy, so the Seventh Air Force looked around for another mission. Fighting had erupted in nearby Cambodia where the political environment was sufficiently permissive for B-57G operations. The Seventh Air Force in July 1971 decided that the B-57Gs would fly normal daytime bombing missions over Cambodia against such targets as storage areas, truck parks, and gun positions. In normal circumstances, each B-57G crew took off against a target or targets chosen by the Seventh Air Force, but before dropping their bombs they rendezvoused with a forward air controller and received a target briefing. After the controller marked the target with smoke, the B-57G dropped its bombs, normally from 4,000 feet above ground level. Many secondary explosions and fires resulted when the bombs hit supplies stacked along the roads, trails, and waterways. Early in September, the squadron began using high-drag Mk-82 bombs to gain an additional 8 seconds of target acquisition time on their 240-knot bomb run.

Some of the Cambodia missions provided much more spectacular results than the single aircraft night attack missions over Laos. When four B-57Gs attacked a target in Cambodia on 9 August 1971, for instance, the first aircraft turned back after encountering intense antiaircraft fire and having one round go through its wing. The next two aircraft also were driven off by intense antiaircraft fire discouraged by the six-eights cloud cover over the target which was too dense for an effective bomb run. The fourth B-57G descended to 4,000 feet, just below the cloud bases, and struck the automatic weapons. The forward air controller confirmed the claim that this fourth aircraft had destroyed all three weapon positions. 32/

(U) Another mission on 11 October pitted a B-57G piloted by Lt. Col. John A. Clark against enemy insurgents attacking allied forces in Cambodia. The forward air controller reported antiaircraft fire along the only possible bomb heading, but the B-57G went in anyway. On the first pass, Colonel Clark and his sensor operator, Capt. Ronald Silvia, destroyed the antiaircraft weapon position, clearing the way for further attacks. The B-57G had just enough fuel to get back to base, but the crew risked another run on which they dropped all remaining ordnance on the enemy mortar and automatic weapons positions that were pinning down the allied ground troops. With the mortars and machineguns silenced, friendly troops broke out of the position and drove off the enemy soldiers. Reports credited the B-57G with killing 150 enemy soldiers, wounding 250, and destroying a number of mortars and machineguns. Even though the B-57G was not intended for normal day bombing, it had that capability and the B-57G crews proved their skill on these hazardous missions. 33/

With the return of the forward looking radar sets and the beginning of the next dry season, the Seventh Air Force ended the day bombing missions over Cambodia on 10 November 1971.34/

(U) Near the end of the rainy season, a personnel crisis came close to crippling the 13th Bombardment Squadron. The maintenance personnel arrived in Thailand as a group in September 1970. Most were new, inexperienced, and suffering from the psychological shock of finding themselves in Southeast Asia. More important to the squadron's long-term operation, however, was the fact they would be eligible to rotate as a group back to the United States in only one year. To preclude such a complete maintenance personnel turnover, the squadron began working with the maintenance squadrons at Takhli Royal Thai Air Force Base which was being closed. By exchanging 20 maintenance specialists, the 13th Bombardment Squadron managed to stagger the rotation dates from June through November 1971, gaining some breathing room. Because replacements normally arrived on or after the scheduled rotation dates, the squadron maintenance force diminished to very dangerous levels. At one time, the squadron had only 26 maintenance personnel assigned against 60 authorized, forcing the maintenance force to work 12-hour shifts, 7 days a week.

(U) Part of the maintenance problem also stemmed from the maintenance concept followed in Southeast Asia. Under the Tactical Air Command's self-contained maintenance concept, the 13th Bombardment Squadron arrived with all of the personnel needed to keep its aircraft flying. PACAF, however, operated under the wing maintenance concept (AFM 66-21) which required most of the specialists to remain with a wing maintenance squadron. This meant that the 13th had to transfer a number of its specialists to the 8th Tactical Fighter

Wing maintenance complex. It also meant that problems once solved locally and quickly, now had to await the arrival of wing specialists.

(U) Most of the problems however ironed themselves out; for example working hours. Except for the brief period where they worked 12 hour shifts, 7 days a week, the squadron worked 12 hours each day for 5 days, and then had a day off. But morale and safety suffered so much that the squadron changed the schedule to six, 8-hour days followed by a day off--a schedule better suited to the temperament of the workers.

Because political arrangements forced the Joint Chiefs of Staff to restrict the Air Force presence in Thailand to a specified number of units and people, General Ryan on 4 August 1971 asked that the 13th Bombardment Squadron be returned to the United States to make room in Thailand for other units which the Air Force considered more essential. General Ryan argued that the 13th had completed its combat evaluation of the B-57G and could hand over its truck killing mission to the AC-130 gunship squadron. In a meeting with Defense Secretary Laird on 10 August 1971, Air Force Secretary Seamans suggested that the 13th Bombardment Squadron remain at Ubon until all 18 AC-130 gunships were operational, probably in January 1972. Secretary Laird on 4 September approved Secretary Seamans' request for a waiver of the Thailand manpower ceiling to allow the Air Force to introduce the scheduled new units while retaining the 13th Bombardment Squadron at Ubon until January 1972. With the manpower ceiling problem resolved, General Ryan withdrew his request for authority to transfer the 13th. [35]

Commando Hunt VII

Monsoon winds again shifted during October 1971 and the dry season began in Laos. Commando Hunt VII, the truckhunting campaign, officially started on 1 November 1971, a week before the Aeronautical Systems Division/Texas Instrument team completed installation of the modified forward looking radar sets in the last of the B-57G aircraft. As previously indicated, the day bombing missions in Cambodia ended on 10 November, and the B-57Gs reverted to night missions along the roads, trails, and waterways of eastern Laos.[36/]

Although flight tests in the United States had predicted that the modified forward looking radar sets would work as planned, the crews soon found the moving target indicator function totally ineffective. Once again the sensor operators had to rely upon the shorter range low light level television and forward looking infrared sensors to detect, identify, and track moving targets. This was more of a handicap than before because many of the sensor operators were new and inexperienced; the original crews had flown the required number of missions and returned to the United States. To add to the difficulties, during the 1971 dry season the Laotian roads dried rather slowly and the enemy increased his truck traffic only gradually. The situation offered a dilemma: lack of traffic allowed the sensor operators more time to train and become proficient with the equipment, but it also meant they had no opportunities to actually acquire targets. Truck hunting was so poor in October 1971 that the B-57Gs destroyed only five trucks. As the truck flow increased and the sensor operators gained confidence, the number of trucks destroyed by the B-57Gs rose to 49 in November and 101 in December. In addition, the B-57G crews in that 3 month period caused 648 secondary explosions and 871 secondary fires in the face of a growing enemy antiaircraft defense that included automatic weapons, guns as large as 85mm, and unguided rockets.37/

While flying its normal night attack missions, the B-57G was reasonably safe from optically sighted antiaircraft because its black-painted underside blended into the night sky. That same color scheme however made the aircraft more visible in daylight than its counterpart with the lighter standard underside camouflage color. This fact became of greater interest to the crews in late November when they began flying two dawn and two dusk missions each day to cover the gaps between day and night missions of the F-4s. During the portions of the missions before dark and after dawn, the black-bottomed aircraft were highly vulnerable to every antiaircraft weapon in the enemy arsenal although there were no losses But the afternoon haze and morning ground fog encountered on those missions adversely affected the sensors, so it was not long before the squadron reverted to night missions only.38/

Secretary Laird had extended the stay of the 13th Bombardment Squadron at Ubon through January 1972, but the Air Force had not decided what to do with the unit after that. Air Force Programming Document 73-3 in June 1971 showed that the B-57Gs were to remain in the active inventory at least through June 1975, but Air Force headquarters on 23 August 1971 indicated that it wanted to transfer them to the Air National Guard by March 1972. Although the Tactical Air Command wanted to keep the aircraft in one of its units, Air Force headquarters on 24 September 1971 changed Programming Document 73-3 to show all of the B-57Gs in the Air National Guard by January 1972. In late November, PACAF alerted the 13th Bombardment Squadron to be ready to return to the United States in December 1971 under Project Corona Condor II. The Air Force consequently held replacement crews at MacDill Air Force Base and diverted replacement maintenance personnel to other units, gradually diminishing the effectiveness of the 13th. The squadron nevertheless continued to fly its scheduled night attack missions over Laos.39/

Combat operations continued on a routine basis when orders for the anticipated December return to the United States failed to arrive. PACAF again alerted the squadron in late February to be ready for return to the United States during May 1972 under Project Pacer Tent. Once more, the Air Force delayed or diverted replacement personnel, causing extremely adverse effects in the maintenance and supply areas. Cracked tailpipes, defective wing fuel cells, and inoperative air-conditioning equipment created high maintenance requirements, further aggravating the maintenance personnel shortage. An acute shortage of spare parts during January forced the squadron to cannibalize one aircraft to keep the others flying, but all aircraft were back in the air during February after the arrival of a shipment of spare parts. Depot-level engine repairs at Clark Air Base were so poor that one aircraft had four different engines installed before engine performance was acceptable for flying. Despite the best efforts of the squadron supply and maintenance personnel, the number of fully operational aircraft declined.40/

Typical of the special missions that interrupted the regular schedule during this period was one on 28 December 1971 to test finned napalm weapons with the B-57G sensor system. One B-57G armed with its normal weapons searched for truck targets while the second aircraft, carrying the test weapons, flew at a much higher altitude. Lt. Col. Edward K. Matthews, the 13th Bombardment

Squadron commander, flew the test aircraft in dive-bombing attacks on targets detected by the other B-57G. Although he destroyed one truck and a 37mm gun, the test was not repeated and the finned napalm did not become a regular B-57G weapon.41/

Another test early in 1972 resulted in a continuing teamwork arrangement between the AC-130 gunships and the B-57Gs. The greater sensor capability of the gunships placed them in the hunter role, while the better ordnance carried by the B-57Gs earned them the killer role against truck convoys, tanks, storage areas, and gun emplacements which the AC-130's guns could not destroy. During Commando Hunt VII, the AC-130 record of trucks destroyed per sortie was three to four times that of each B-57G sortie. Working as a team, however, the two aircraft destroyed targets that either working alone could not have attacked.42/

Recording and confirming target destruction became one of the B-57Gs most frustrating tasks. The effort to automate the process by installing video recorders in two B-57Gs at Ubon for tests under combat conditions had failed, so in March 1972 the Westinghouse engineer removed the recorders from the test aircraft and returned the cameras, spare parts, tools, data, and residual film rolls to the Aeronautical Systems Division.43/ The squadron continued to claim target destruction, but had no dependable method of proving this.

Claims for target destruction during the January to March 1972 period were significantly higher than for the preceding 3 month period. The 13th Bombardment Squadron noted destruction of 369 trucks, two 37mm guns, two 57mm guns, a tracked vehicle, and three tanks. In addition, it made two roads cuts and caused 1,474 secondary explosions and 1,255 fires. The explosions and fires probably destroyed many more trucks, but there was no way to verify that fact.44/ The squadron had run up a commendable record in what was to prove to be its final months.

VI -- TERMINATION OF TROPIC MOON III, AND SUMMARY

Return to the United States

Orders came at last directing the squadron to move its aircraft to Forbes AFB, Kansas, on 10 April 1972. The squadron flew 69 night attack sorties in the Steel Tiger portion of Laos between 1 and 10 April, destroying 12 trucks in its final days of combat. The B-57Gs left Ubon Royal Thai Air Force Base on 12 April 1972, en route to Clark Air Base on the first leg of the return to the United States. 1/

In a final effort to keep the B-57Gs available, Adm. John S. McCain Jr., Commander-in-Chief, Pacific, asked General Clay, CINCPACAF, to hold the aircraft at Clark Air Base for possible return to the war if the North Vietnamese offensive continued to accelerate. Among his several reasons for not holding the aircraft, General Clay cited the fact that only the aircraft and flight crews remained, all support personnel having left; the delay (freeze) would cause severe turbulence throughout the Air Force, particularly in the personnel system, and the unsettled weather expected along the ferry route after mid-May would endanger the aircraft needlessly. Admiral McCain accepted General Clay's reasoning, and on 21 April the Joint Chiefs of Staff told the Air Force to continue the move to the United States. The Tactical Air Command on 20 April 1972 cancelled TAC ROC 62-67, which 4 years earlier had generated the original Tropic Moon III actions. The first jet-powered, self-contained, night attack aircraft program was over. 2/

Although all aircraft, equipment, and personnel had been transferred, the 13th Bombardment Squadron, Tactical, on paper remained at Ubon Royal Thai Air Force Base. Pacific Air Forces moved it to Clark Air Base on 24 December and assigned it to the 405th Fighter Wing, still without personnel or equipment. The Air Force redesignated the squadron the 13th Fighter Squadron on 1 July 1973, but before finally inactivated it on 30 September 1973, PACAF first redesignated it the 13th Bombardment Squadron, Tactical.3/ This did not mark the end of B-57G activity, however, because they were headed for the Air National Guard.

The Air National Guard

By June 1972, the 190th Tactical Bombardment Squadron, Air National Guard, at Forbes AFB, Kansas, had fourteen B-57G aircraft-- 10 returned from Southeast Asia and 4 transferred from MacDill Air Force Base. The Air Force had provided 42 active duty personnel and 5 contractor technicians to assist the Air National Guard during the transition to the B-57G, and maintenance personnel were reinstalling the sensors and equipment that had been removed for the ferry flight from Southeast Asia. While the transition proceeded, the Air Staff took one more look at the B-57G.4/

On 19 June 1972, the Tactical Division, Deputy Chief of Staff for Plans and Operations, at Air Force headquarters summarized the Air Force's reasons for leaving the B-57Gs with the Air National Guard. Most significantly, such action kept the aircraft and support equipment in a combat-ready status and available for any short-notice contingency that might arise. Keeping the aircraft operational also insured the availability of vehicles for continued evaluation of the various sensors and techniques associated with self-contained night attack technoloby. The active duty and National Guard personnel assigned to the squadron formed a pool of trained technicians to support the system should it be needed in a combat situation. All of those factors supported the Secretary of Defense's policy of providing the Air National Guard with modern equipment and meaningful missions. Finally, keeping the B-57Gs active averted undesirable political reactions that might result from the early phaseout of such a widely publicized and expensive system.[5/]

Not everyone accepted or agreed with those reasons. General Eade preferred to retire the B-57Gs to storage at Davis-Monthan Air Force Base, but conceded that if the Air National Guard needed the airframes just for something to fly, they could keep the B-57Gs until something better became available.[6/]

Eight general officers from Air Force headquarters met on 23 June 1972 to determine the final disposition of the B-57G aircraft. Maj. Gen. Donovan F. Smith, Assistant Deputy Chief of Staff for Plans and Operations, presented General Eade's suggestion that the Air Force place the B-57Gs in storage, but Lt. Gen. George S. Boylan, Deputy Chief of Staff for Programs and Resources, argued in favor of keeping them in the Air National Guard. After evaluating both agruments, Gen. Horace M. Wade, Vice Chief of Staff, decided that the B-57Gs should remain in the Air National Guard, at least for a time.[7/] In early 1974, however, the Air National Guard delivered all of the B-57Gs to Davis-Monthan Air Force Base for storage.

Summary

After spending 4 months deciding to create the B-57G, the Air Force took 6 months to identify the necessary funds and 27 months to modify and test the aircraft. Those 37 months of preparation yielded 18 months of combat. Throughout the program, the B-57G had advocates such as General Schinz and the Southeast Asia Projects Division, and such opponents as General Momyer, who interposed objections in 1968 and again in 1970. The B-57G emerged from a high priority program directed by the Air Staff that circumvented at least half of the Air Force Systems Command's normal development cycle. Because the B-57G was the only tactical bomber in the Air Force inventory, the development program was monitored by a systems project office whose usual primary concern was cargo aircraft.

The B-57G never equaled expectations. The airframe measured up to the planning criteria, but the sensors and associated equipment failed in most respects. The B-57G cost twice the estimated $52 million, and the expected 18 months from contract award to deployment stretched to 27 months. Because the moving target indicator feature of its radar never functioned, the B-57G had no long-range sensor. And finally, the B-57G never achieved the promised kill rate of 6.9 trucks per sortie and 79 trucks per day.

NOTES TO CHAPTER I

Notes to pages 1 to 7

1. Study (U), Historical Division, AU, 1953, <u>Development of Night Air Operations, 1941-1952</u>. Study No. 101-92, p. 109.

2. <u>Ibid</u>, pp. 134, 138.

3. During World War II, the Army Air Forces used the Martin B-26 Marauder and the Douglas A-26. The Martin B-26 was removed from service after the war, and a realignment of aircraft designators changed the Douglas A-26 to the B-26. The latter served in Korea and in Southeast Asia in limited numbers.

4. Study (S/XGDS), HQ USAF, <u>Operation Shed Light</u>, pp. 1A-5 to 1A-6; rprt (S), 7AF, <u>Night Airborne Search Operations in Southeast Asia</u>, undated, pp. 1, 3.

5. Study (S/XGDS), HQ USAF, <u>Operation Shed Light</u>, pp 1D-99, 1D-103; study (S/NOFORN), <u>Development of All-Weather and Night Truck Kill Capability</u>, Project CORONA HARVEST Special Report No. 70-14, January 1970, p. 7.

6. Study (S/XGDS), HQ USAF, <u>Operation Shed Light</u>, p. 1D-101; rprt, (S), 7AF, <u>Night Airborne Search Operations in Southeast Asia</u>, undated, pp. 4, 5.

7. Pentagon Papers (U), GPO Edition, VI, Air War in North Vietnam, I, pp. 56-57; memo (S), Dr. Vincent V. McRae, President's Science Advisor Staff to Science Advisor, subj: Case Study for the Vietnam Development Group, <u>Night Vision for Aircraft Systems</u>, 13 Dec 67, p. 2.

8. Memo (S), McRae to Science Advisor, 13 Dec 67, pp. 1-2.

9. <u>Ibid</u>., p. 2; hist (S), Dir of Development, Jul-Dec 66, pp. 93-94.

10. Hist (S), Director of Development, Jul-Dec 66, p. 95.

11. Hist (S), ASD, Jan-Dec 66, I, pp. 158-160; hist (S), Dir of Development, Jul-Dec 66, pp. 94-96; ltr (U), Gen. John P. McConnell, CSAF, to AFSC, subj: Operation Shed Light, 15 Jul 66.

12. Hist (S), Dir of Development, Jul-Dec 66, p. 3; Staff Study (U), Maj. James R. Patterson, Jr., SEA Proj Division, subj: Operation Shed Light, undated, p. 9.

Notes to pages 8 to 11

13. Memo (S), Sec of Air Force Brown to DCS/Plans and Ops, 8 Aug 66; memo (S), Sec Brown to Sec Def, subj: Questions Resulting from Briefing on USAF Night Operations in SEA, 24 Aug 66; memo (S), Gen. McConnell, CSAF, to Dep Sec Def, 25 Aug 66; msg (S/AFEO), CSAF to PACAF, AFXO 76796, 28 Sep 66.

14. Msg (C/AFEO), CINCPACAF to 7AF, DOP, 30445 Oct 66, 221820Z Oct 66.

15. Msg (C/AFEO), 7AF to CINCPACAF, C-66-TS 20518 Nov 66, 240655Z Nov 66.

16. Hist (S), AFSC, Jul 66-Jun 67, I, p. 3; hist (S), ASD, Jan-Dec 66, I, pp. 160-161; msg (S), CSAF to ASD, AFRDD-S 89798, 6 Dec 66; hist (S), Dir of Dev, Jul-Dec 66, pp. 96-98; hist (S) Dir of Dev, Jan-Jun 67, pp. 105-107; memo (C), Harry Davis, Dep Asst SAF R&D (Special Programs), subj: USAF FY 76 RDT&E Funds for Operation Shed Light, Self-Contained Night-Attack System, 30 Sep 66; memo (C), Dr. Alexander Flax, Asst SAF R&D to DDR&E, subj: Air Force Operation Shed Light, 2 Aug 66; memo (S), Dr. John S. Foster, DDR&E to Asst SAF R&D, subj: Guidance on Air Force Proposed Operation Shed Light, 20 Sep 66.

17. Rprt (S), Symposium to Consider Army-Navy-Air Force Problems on the Vietnam War, 16-18 Feb 66, pp. 6ff.

18. Hist (S), TAWC, Jan-Jun 67, I, pp. 45-46; hist (S), AFSC, Jul 66-Jun 67, I, p. 3; hist (S), ASD, Jan-Dec 66, I, pp. 160-161; msg (S), CSAF to ASD, AFRDD-S 89798, 6 Dec 66; hist (S), Dir of Dev, memo (C), Dr. Alexander Flax, Asst SAF R&D, to DDR&E, subj: Air Force Operation Shed Light, 2 Aug 66; memo (S), Dr. John S. Foster, DDR&E, to Asst SAF R&D, subj: Guidance on Air Force Proposed Operation Shed Light, 20 Sep 66.

19. Memo (S), McRae to Science Advisor, 13 Dec 67, p. 2; hist (S), Dir of Development, Jul-Dec 66, pp. 93-94.

20. Hist (S), ASD, Jan-Dec 66, I, pp. 162, 178-179.

21. Memo (C), SEA Action Item, II-S, atch to ltr Vice C/S to SAF, 28 Feb 67; hist (S), Dir of Dev, DCSAF, HQ USAF, Jan-Jun 67, I, p. 103.

22. 7AF SEAOR #117, 7 Apr 66; hist (S), Dir of Dev, Jan-Jun 67, I, pp. 103, 106, and Jul-Dec 67, I, pp. 180-181; hist (S), TAC, Jul-Dec 67, pp. 272-279.

NOTES TO CHAPTER II

Notes to pages 12 to 16

1. Hist (S), Dir of Dev, Jul-Dec 67, pp. 175-176; hist (S), TAC, Jul-Dec 67, pp. 280-282; Background Paper (S), Tropic Moon III History, AFSC, 12 Aug 70.

2. AFSCM 375-4, 31 May 66, p. 1; msg (S), CSAF to AFSC, AFRDDH 75852, 17 Oct 67.

3. Msg (S), CSAF to AFSC, AFRDDH 75852, 17 Oct 67; referral sheed (U), Maj. Gen. Joseph J. Cody, Jr., Do AFSC/SCS, SCGA, and SCL, 18 Oct 67; memo (S), Lt. Col. Leighton Palmerton to Lt. Gen. Otto J. Glasser, DCS/R&D, subj: Genesis of B-57G Program, Aug 70.

4. TAC ROC 62-67 (S), 7 Nov 67; msg (S), AFSC to ASD, 082025Z Nov 67; rprt (U), TAC (TAWC), B-57G Program Category III Test, Jan 71, p. iii.

5. Ltr (S), Mr. James A Reamer, Jr., ASD to 7AF, PACAF, and AFSC, subj: Tropic Moon III, 23 Dec 67; hist (S), Dir of Dev, Jul-Dec 67, pp. 204-205; atch (S), to ltr (U), Col. Roger D. Coleson, AFCUSB, to AFCHO, subj: Monthly Historical Rprts, undated; Chronology (S), Lt. Col. Weedlun, SEA Proj Div, subj: Tropic Moon III, undated.

6. Rprt (S/NOFORN/GDS-3), <u>The Basis for Configuring a Tropic Moon III System with an Analysis of Its Effectiveness</u>, DCS/R&D, SEA Proj Div, p. iv; rprt (S), John L. Davis, ANSER, Inc., <u>Effectiveness Analysis for Tropic Moon III</u>, Jan 68, pp. v-vii.

7. Study (S/XGDS), HQ USAF, Operation Shed Light, p. 1D-35; rprt (S/NOFORN/GDS-3), <u>The Basis for Configuring A Tropic Moon III System with an Analysis of Its Effectiveness</u>, DCS/R&D, HQ USAF, Dec 67, p. 31.

8. Hist (S), Dir of Dev, Jul-Dec 67, pp. 180-183; hist (S), TAC, Jul-Dec 67, pp. 269-272; rprt (S), TAWC, subj: TAC Test 67-16, Tropic Moon II (SEA Phase), Jul 68, p. i; brgs (S), Col. Louis C. Wright, SEA Proj Div to PSAC, subj: Air Force Shed Light Program, 30 Nov 67.

9. SOW (S), TM-III, 1 Mar 68; Status Rprt (S), SEA Proj. Div, subj: Tropic Moon III, 1 Dec 67; MR (S), SEA Proj Div, subj: Tropic Moon III, 20 Dec 67; msg (S), AFSC to ASD, 201958Z Nov 67.

10. SOW (S), TM-III, 1 Mar 68, pp. 1-2, and atch 17, 18 (C).

Notes to pages 18 to 22

11. Ibid; rprt (S/NOFORN/GDS-3), DCS/R&D, HQ USAF, Dec 67, p. 32.

12. Atch 3 to SOW (S), TM-III, 1 Mar 68, pp. 1-3, 10-12; atch 4 (C) to SOW, pp. 1-3; atch 5 (C) to SOW, p. 1; atch 6 (C) to SOW, pp. 1, 6; atch 7 to SOW.

13. SOW (S), TM-III, 1 Mar 68, pp. 62, 65, 68-69, 73.

14. Ltr (S), McConnell to SAF, 5 Feb 68; ltr (S), Flax to CSAF, 3 Feb 68; ltr (S), Flax to SAF, subj: B-57 Night Attack Aircraft Program, 10 Feb 68; memo (S), Brown to Sec Def, 12 Feb 68; memo (S), Deputy Sec Def Paul R. Nitze to SAF, subj: B-57 Night Attack Aircraft Program, 24 Feb 68; ltr (S), James R. Leist, Jr., ASD to contractors, 8 Mar 68.

15. PCR (S), SAF to Sec Def, F-8-014, subj: Tactical Auxiliary Forces (B-57 Tropic Moon III), 1 Mar 68; memo (S), Lt. Col Palmerton, SEA Proj Div, to Gen. Glasser, undated, p. 2; hist (S), Modification Requirements (S), Dir/Opnl Req and Dev Plans, #1959, 8 May 68; rprt (S), C-141/C-130 SPO, subj: Tropic Moon III Significant Program Events through 31 Dec 68, p. 5 (hereinafter cited as SPO Chronos Chronos . . .); AFR 57-4.

16. Hist (S), Dir of Dev, Jul-Dec 67, pp. 198-199; rprt (S), TAWC, TAC Test 67-16, Tropic Moon III (SEA Phase), Jul 68, p. i; trip report (S), Lt. Col, J.R. Smith, 7AF, 10 May 68; ltr (S), Gen. Momyer, 7AF to Gen. Ferguson, AFSC, 14 Mar 68; ltr (S), Gen. Gerguson to Gen. Momyer, 9 Apr 68.

17. SPO Chronos through 31 Dec 68, pp. 6-7; memo (S), Lt. Col. Palmerton to Gen. Glasser, undated, p. 3; msg (S), PACAF to 7AF, DO 028, 8 Jun 68; staff summary sheet (S), 7AF, 8 Jun 68; msg (S), CSAF to PACAF and TAC, 182042Z Jun 68; hist (S), TAC, Jan-Jun 68, pp. 280-281; ltr (S), Lt. Gen. Harry Goldsworthy, DCS/Systems and Logistics, to CSAF, Nov 70; hist (S), Dir of Dev, Jan-Jun 68, pp. 176-177.

18. Memo (S), Lt. Col. Palmerton to Gen. Glasser, undated, p. 3; SPO Chrons (S), through 31 Dec 68, p. 7; S.O. A-504, ASD, 25 Apr 68.

19. Ltr (S), Gen. Ferguson, AFSC, to Gen Momyer, 7AF, 1 Jul 68; ltr (S), Gen. Momyer to Gen. Ferguson, 10 Jul 68; hist (S), Dir of Dev, Jul-Dec 68, p. 169.

NOTES TO CHAPTER III

Notes to pages 25 to 32

1. Study (S/NOFORN/AFEO/XGDS), AMC, History of the B-57 Airplane, July 1953-January 1958, Historical Study No. 316, Sep 58 Frederick A. Alling.

2. Plan (S/NOFORN/XGDS), MATS Programming Plan for Conversion & Equipping MATS Units with RB-57F Aircraft, 28 Nov 63, in hist (S/NOFORN/XGDS), MATS, Jul-Dec 63, IV, II-56.

3. Amendment 1 (S) to Modification Requirement 1959, Dir/Opnl Req and Dev Plans, 14 Aug 68; hist (S), Dir of Dev, Jul-Dec 68, pp. 169-170; hist (S), ASD, FY-70, I, p. 163; SPO Chronos (S), through 31 Dec 68, pp. 7-8; msg (U), CSAF to PACAF et al, 241615Z Oct 68; Development Directive (C), DD #207, subj: Hayes Dispenser Qualifications on the B-57, 25 Jul 68.

4. Ltr (S), HQ USAF to TAC, 21 Jan 69; subj: Activation of 13th Bombardment Squadron, Tactical; TAC general order 12, 23 Jan 69.

5. Ltr, (S), CSAF to PACAF et al, 302012Z Jan 69; hist (S), Dir of Dev, Jan-Jun 68, p. 180; ltr (S), Maj. Gen. Goldsworthy to AFSC, subj: B-57G Program Change Study, 69-ASZL-73, 1 Apr 69; extract (S) from hist (TS), DCS/Ops, Jan-Jun 69, p. 285; hist (S), TAC FY-71, pp. 281-282; ltr (S), Maj. Gen. Zoeckler, AFSC, to HQ USAF, subj: B-57G Program Change, 9 May 69.

6. Ltr (C), DDR&E to Asst Sec Army (R&D), Navy (R&D), Air Force (R&D), subj: Effective Air Armament for Truck Interdiction, 23 May 69.

7. Report (S), Maj. Robert P. Lavoie, AFSC, subj: B-57G Program Review at Westinghouse, 15-16 Jul 69, undated; minutes (S), B-57G Conference at Eglin AFB, 15-17 Sep 69; SPO Chronos (S), Jul-Dec 69; msg (S), CSAF to AFSC, 011634Z Aug 69.

8. Atch (S) to Memo, Col. William Y. Smith to SAF, subj: Gunships, 7 Nov 69.

9. Hist (S), Dir of Dev, Jul-Dec 69, pp. 192-193; SPO Chronos (S), Jul-Dec 69, p.5; hist (S), ASD, FY-70, I, p. 164; SPO Chronos (S), Jan-Jun 70, p. 1.

10. SPO Chronos (S), Jan-Jun 70, pp. 1-3; hist (S), TAC, FY-71, pp. 283-284; hist (S), Dir of Dev & Acq, Jan-Jun 70, pp. 148-149.

11. SPO Chronos (S), Jan-Jun 70, pp. 2-7.

12. Ibid, pp. 9-12; hist (S), Dir of Dev & Acq, Jan-Jun 70, p. 148.

Notes to pages 32 to 39

13. Rprt (S), ADTC, TR-70-145, subj: Compatibility of Selected Munitions with the B-57G Aircraft, Aug 70; rprt (U), ADTC TR-70-162, subj: Compatibility of the Modular Bomb Dispenser on the B-57G Aircraft, Aug 70; Rprt (S), ADTC, TR-70-150, subj: Engineering Evaluation of the B-57 Aircraft/Mk-82 Laser Guided Bomb System, Aug 70.

14. WRAMA Historical Study #23, Tropic Moon III: The B-57G Canberra, 1968-1971, hist office, WRAMA, Jul 71, pp. 19-22, 27, 29, 31.

15. Msg (S), TAC to AFSC, 132220Z Jul 70.

16. SPO Chronos (S), Jan-Jun 70, pp. 10-12; hist (S), Dir of Dev & Acq, Jan-Jun 70, p. 149.

17. Ibid.

18. Rprt (S), ADTC, TR-71-81, subj: B-57G Category II Test, Jun 71; SPO Chronos (S), Jan-Jun 70, pp. 9-11.

19. Hist (S), ASD, FY-70, I, p. 167.

20. Report (S), TAWC, subj: B-57G Program Category III Test, Jan 71.

21. Rprt (S), Maj. Douglas J. Kosan, subj: Category III Test (subjective) on B-57G, 2 Aug 70, pp. 5-6.

22. SPO Chronos (S), Jul-Dec 70, p. 1; msg (S) Tac to AFSC, 132220Z Jul 70; msg (S), AFSC to TAC and AFLC, 151700Z Jul 70; msg (S), TAC to CSAF, AFSC, AFLC, 161700Z Jul 70.

23. Msg (S), CSAF to TAC, AFSC, AFLC, 181736Z Jul 70.

24. Msg (S), CSAF to PACAF, 081456Z Aug 70; msg (S), PACAF to CSAF, 101911Z Aug 70; MR (S), Brig. Gen. Carroll H. Bolender, Dep Dir Dev & Acq, subj: Briefing to Chief of Staff, 12 Aug 70; MR (S), SEA Proj Div, subj: 13th BST Status, 12 Aug 70.

25. SPO Chronos (S), Jul-Dec 70, p. 2; minutes (S), B-57G Meeting at MacDill AFB, 21-22 Jul 70.

26. Ltr (S), Gen. John C. Meyer to Gen. James Ferguson, subj: Program Management, 10 Aug 70; Background Paper (S), AFSC/SDR, subj: Tropic Moon III, 12 Aug 70.

Notes to pages 39 to 40

27. Background Paper (S), AFSC/SDR, subj: Tropic Moon III, 12 Aug 70.

28. SPO Chronos (S), Jul-Dec 70, p. 3; WRAMA Historical Study #23, pp. 33-34, 37-39, 187-203; munites (S), B-57G Meetings at MacDill AFB, 20 Aug 70 and 26 Aug 70; msg (S), CSAF to PACAF, 191919Z Aug 70.

29. Msg (S), TAC to CSAF, 022300Z Sep 70; CSAF Decision (S), atch to memo (S), Col. V.J. DeArmond, Dir, AF Board Structure, to AFCHO, 15 Oct 70; hist (S), 13 BST, Oct-Dec 70, pp. 2-4.

NOTES TO CHAPTER IV

Notes to pages 41 to 45

1. SPO Chronos (S), Jul-Dec 70, pp. 6-7; msg (S), 8 TFW to 13AF, 030340Z Nov 70; mmsg (S), 13AF to PACAF, 060815Z Nov 70; msg (S), PACAF to AFLC, et al, 060330Z Nov 70.

2. SPO Chronos (S), Jul-Dec 70, p. 7; Management Plan (S), ASD, B-57G Radar Remedial Program, 2 Feb 71, pp. 6-7; hist (S), 13th BST, Oct-Dec 70, p. 10.

3. Trip Report (S), Texas Instruments, 13 Dec 70; WRAMA Historical Study #23 (S), pp. 109-110; hist (S), Dir/Maint Eng, Jul-Dec 70, p. 68; Management Plan, ASD, B-57G Radar Remedial Program, 2 Feb 71, pp. 5-6.

4. MR (S), Maj. Everett T. Taspberry, Dir/Ops, 15 Dec 70; Management Plan (S), ASD, B-57G Radar Remedial Program, 2 Feb 71, pp. 6-7.

5. SPO Chronos (S), Jan-Jun 71, pp. 3-5; hist (S), Dir/Maint Eng, Jan-Jun 71, p. 57; munites (S), 24 May Special Quad Directors Coordinating Meeting. (U) On 24 May 1971, Air Force headquarters learned that AFSC had intended a 17 May request for $14.892 million to cover unaudited over-target costs of $4.64 million, contractor claims of $6.552 million, and $3.7 million for the radar remedial program and other improvement projects. Air Force headquarters saved $700,000 by ordering the radar remedial testing program ended by 15 June, and added $3 million to the improvement program. The total B-57G spending thus came to $99,770,755 but could go much higher if the Air Force approved existing contractor claims. Spending on the B-57G came to a temporary halt when Air Force headquarters told AFSC to obtain approval before committing any additional funds.

6. Munites (C), B-57G Program Review Meeting, 13-14 May 71, undated.

7. Report (S), ADTC, TR-71-81, Supp 1, subj: B-57G Category II Test (B-57G AN/APQ-139 Radar Test), Aug 71, pp. 1, 607, 12-22.

8. SPO Chronos (S), Jul-Dec 71, pp. 3-9; hist (S), 13 BST, Jul-Sep 71, p. 5, and Oct-Dec 71, Ch. III.

9. Hist (S), Acq & Test Div, Jul-Dec 68, p. 249,; msg (S), PACAF to CSAF, 092145Z Apr 68; msg (S), AFSC to CSAF, 031702Z Jun 68; hist (S), Dir of Dev, Jan-Jun 68, p. 177, and Jul-Dec 68, p. 170.

Notes to pages 47 to 53

10. Hist (S), ASD, FY-69, I, p. 143, and FY-70, I, pp. 168-169; hist (S), Dir of Dev, Jan-Jun 69, pp. 181-182, and Jul-Dec 69, pp. 193-194, and Jan-Jun 70, pp. 149-150.

11. Hist (S), Dir of Dev, Jul-Dec 68, p. 170, and Jan-Jun 70, pp. 149-150; hist (S), ASD, FY-70, I, pp. 169-170.

12. Hist (S), ASD, FY-70, I, pp. 168, 170-173; hist (S), Dir of Dev, Jan-Jun 70, pp. 149-150, and Jul-Dec 70, p. 114, and Jan-Jun 71, p. 112.

13. Hist (S), Dir of Dev, Jan-Jun 71, pp. 112-114.

14. Report (C), ADTC, TR-71-147, subj: B-57G Pave Gat Category II Test, Dec 71.

15. Ibid.

16. Msg (U), ASD to AFSC, 042106Z Aug 71; msg (S), 7AF to PACAF, 061045Z Oct 71; msg (S), 13AF to PACAF, 070805A Oct 71; msg (C) AFSC to CSAF, 011530Z Dec 71; SPO Chronos (S), Jul-Dec 71, pp. 10-11; msg (S), CSAF to PACAF, 131343Z Dec 71; msg (S), PACAF to CSAF, 142157Z Dec 71; msg (S), CSAF to PACAF, 212136Z Dec 71.

17. Report (S), TAWC #71A-066T, subj: Combat Evaluation, B-57G, Mar 71; msg (C), CSAF to AFSC and PACAF, 021240Z Mar 71; msg (C), ASD to AFSC, 152040Z Mar 71; msg (C), PACAF to CSAF, 240057Z Mar 71; msg (U), CSAF to AFSC and PACAF, 312309Z Mar 71.

18. Msg (U), ASD to AFSC, et. al., 191614Z Apr 71; msg (U), ASD to AFSC, 061804Z May 71; msg (U), AFSC to CSAF, 101715Z May 71; msg (C), CSAF to AFSC, 131505Z May 71.

19. SPO Chronos (S), Jul-Dec 71, pp. 3, 609; msg (C), 8TFW to 13AF, 020901Z Oct 71; hist (S), Dir of Opnl Test & Eval, Jul-Dec 71, p. 259; MR (C), SEA Proj Div, subj: Video Recorder for B-57G, undated.

20. Hist (S), 13 BST, Oct-Dec 71, Ch. III; msg (C), PACAF to CSAF, 142125Z Feb 72; msg (C), AFSC to PACAF, 151900Z Feb 72; msg (C), CSAF to ASD, et. al., 172300Z Feb 72, ltr (C), AFSC to CSAF, subj: B-57G BDA Recorder, 3 Mar 72; msg (U), 8TFW to 13AF, 041208Z Mar 72.

21. Msg (S), 7AF to PACAF, et. al., 180201Z Jul 70; msg (S), PACAF to CSAF, et. al., 231852Z Jul 70; msg (S), PACAF to CSAF, et. al., 132325Z Aug 71.

Notes to pages 53 to 54

22. Msg (S), CSAF to PACAF, et. al., 042146Z Nov 70; msg (S), 7AF to PACAF, et. al., 160201Z Nov 70; msg (S), PACAF to CSAF, et. al., 162042Z Nov 70; hist (S), 7AF, Jan-Jun 71, pp. 212-213.

23. Staff Summary Sheet (U), 7AF, subj: B-57G ECM Configuration, 30 Oct 70; msg (S), 7AF to 7/13AF, 310930Z Oct 70; msg (S), 8TFW to 7AF, 05

24. Ltr (C), Texas Instruments to ASD; 12 Feb 71; ltr (U), Texas Instruments to ASD, 16 Apr 71; ltr (U), Maj. Victor E. Yoakum, ASD, to Texas Instruments, 21 Jul 71.

25. Msg (S), AFSC to 7AF, 231440Z Dec 70; msg (S), 7AF to AFSC, 280010Z Dec 70; ltr (S), Dr. David to Secretary Seamans, 28 May 71.

NOTES TO CHAPTER V

Notes to pages 56 to 66

1. TAC S.O. G-12, 23 Jan 69; hist (C), 15th TFW, Jan-Jun 69, Atch 3, and Jul-Sep 69, Atch 2, hist of 13 BST, and Oct-Dec 69, Atch 2, hist of 13 BST.

2. Hist (C), 15th TFW, Jul-Sep 69, Atch 2, hist of 13 BST, and Oct-Dec 69, Atch 2, hist of 13 BST; hist (U), 15 TFW, Jul-Sep 70, p. 30.

3. Msg (S), TAC to TAWC et. al., 171850Z Jul 70; msg (S), TAC to TAWC et. al., 201335Z Jul 70.

4. Ltr (U) to Rep. James A. Haley, 7th Dist, Florida, 24 Jul 70; ltr (U), Rep. Haley to Rep. Mendel Rivers, Chairman, House Armed Services Committee, and to Office of Legislative Liaison, HQ USAF, 4 Aug 70; ltr (U), Rep. Rivers to GAO, 6 Aug 70; ltr (U), Mr. James H. Hammond, Assoc Dir, GAO, to Sec Def, 18 Aug 70; memo (S), Col. Howard W. Leaf, SEA Proj Div, to Maj. Gen. David V. Miller, Dir Dev & Acq, and Brig. Gen. Carroll H. Bollender, Dep Dir Dev & Acq, subj: GAO Investigation of B-57G Program, 18 Aug 70; MR (S), Col. Howard W. Leaf, subj: GAO Visit to 13 BST, MacDill AFB, 27 Aug 70, 28 Aug 70; ltr (S), Maj. Gen. John C. Giraudo, Dir Leg Liaison, to Rep. Mendel Rivers, 27 Aug 70; MR (S/AFEO), Col. Howard W. Leaf, 11 Sep 70.

5. Msg (S), TAC to TAWC et. al., 171850Z Jul 70; msg (C), AFSC to TAC et. al., 081952Z Sep 70.

6. Msg (S), TAC to CSAF et. al., 022300Z Sep 70.

7. Ibid.

8. Msg (C), CSAF to 13 BST, 142023Z Sep 70; hist (S/NOFORN), 8th TFW, Jul-Sep 70, I, pp. 20-21, and Oct-Dec 70, III, hist of 13 BST, p. 1.

9. Hist (S/NOFORN/Gp-3), 8 TFW, Oct-Dec 70, III, Hist of 13 BST, pp. 2-3, 14-15.

10. Maj. Louis Seig, Impact of Geography on Air Operations In SEA, (S)(HQ PACAF, Project CHECO, 11 Jun 70), pp. 6-7; rprt (S/NOFORN), 7AF, subj: Commando Hunt V, May 71, pp. 1-4.

Notes to pages 66 to 76

11. Msg (S), TAC to CSAF, et. al., 022300Z Sep 70.

12. SPO Chronos (S), Jul-Dec 70, pp. 5-7; extract (S), hist (TS), DCS/Ops, Jul-Dec 70, p. 269; hist (S/NOFORN/Gp-3), 8TFW, Oct-Dec 70, I, pp. 35-36.

13. Report (S/NOFORN), 7AF, subj: Commando Hunt V, May 71, p. 61; hist (S/NOFORN/Gp-3), 8TFW, Oct-Dec 70, I, p. 40; rprt (S/GDS-3) TAC, TAWC First Report, B-57G SEA Combat Evaluation, Mar 71.

14. As in Note 13.

15. As in Note 13.

16. Hist (S/NOFORN/Gp-3), 8TFW, Oct-Dec 70, I, pp. 38-39.

17. Ibid.

18. Hist (S/NOFORN/Gp-3), 8TFW, Oct-Dec 71, I, pp. 37-39, and Jan-Mar 71, I, p. 36.

19. Hist (S/NOFORN/Gp-3), 8TFW, Jan-Mar 71, III, hist of 13 BST, p. 5.

20. Msg (S/NOFORN), 8TFW to PACAF, et. al., 131500Z Dec 70; hist (S/NOFORN/Gp-3), 8TFW, Oct-Dec 70, I, pp. 34, 46, and II, Atch 11, and III, hist of 13 BST, pp. 15-16.

21. Study (S), WRAMA Historical Study #23, pp. 68-70; msg (S/NOFORN), 8TFW to PACAF, et. al., 041516Z Dec 70; SPO Chronos (S), Jul-Dec 70, pp. 8-10; Management Summary (S), Dir/Mgt Anal, subj: Southeast Asia, 17 Mar 71, p. SEA 3; hist (S/NOFORN/Gp-3), 8TFW, Oct-Dec 70, III, hist of 13 BST, p. 16.

22. Hist (S/NOFORN/Gp-3), 8TFW, Oct-Dec 70, III, hist of 13 BST, p. 12, and Jan-Mar 71, III, hist of 13 BST, p. 10, and Apr-Jun 71, III, hist of 13 BST, and Jul-Sep 71, III, hist of 13 BST, p. 13.

23. Study (S), WRAMA Historical Study #23, pp. 87-88, 112, 119; msg (C), WRAMA to PACAF, 102216Z Nov 70; hist (S/NOFORN/Gp-3), 8TFW, Jan-Mar 71, I, pp. 39-40.

24. Hist (S/NOFORN/Gp-3), 8TFW, Jan-Mar 71, I, p. 35.

25. Hist (S/NOFORN/Gp-3), 8TFW, Oct-Dec 71, I, p. 54, and Jan-Mar 72, hist of 13 BST, and Jul-Sep 71, I, p. 53.

Notes to pages 77 60 88

26. Hist (S/NOFORN/Gp-3), 8TFW, Jan-Mar 71, I, p. 37.

27. Hist (S/NOFORN/Gp-3), 8TFW, Oct-Dec 70, III, hist of 13 BST, p. 11.

28. Hist (S/NOFORN/Gp-3), 8TFW, Jan-Mar 71, I, pp. 38-39, and Apr-Jun 71, I, pp. 45-46.

29. Hist (S/NOFORN/Gp-3), 8TFW, Jul-Sep 71, I, pp. 53-55.

30. Hist (S), 13 BST, Apr-Jun 71, pp. 8-9; hist (S), 13 BST, Jul-Sep 71, pp. 11-12.

31. Hist (S/NOFORN/Gp-3), 8TFW, Jul-Sep 71, I, p. 57.

32. Ibid., pp. 58-60.

33. Ibid., p. 61.

34. Paper (S), Lt. Col. Doty, DCS/R&D, subj: B-57G Pave Gat, 13 Oct 71; Item of Interest (S), Lt. Col. Robert G. Morrison, Tactical Div, subj: B-57G Redeployment to CONUS, 5 Aug 71; staff study (S), Col. Morrison, subj: B-57G Disposition, 26 Aug 70; memo (S), SAF to Sec Def, subj: Military Manpower Ceilings in Thailand, 17 Aug 71; hist (S/NOFORN/Gp-3), 8TFW, Jul-Sep 71, III, hist of 13 BST, pp. 18-19.

35. Hist (S/NOFORN/Gp-3), 8TFW, Jul-Sep 71, I, p. 57.

36. Talking Paper (S), Col. Doty, subj: B-57G Pave Gat, 13 Oct 71; staff study (S), Col. Morrison, subj: B-57G Disposition, 26 Aug 71; hist (S/NOFORN/Gp-3), 8TFW, Oct-Dec 71, I, p. 52.

37. Hist (S/NOFORN/Gp-3), 8TFW, Oct-Dec 71, I, p. 59.

38. Ibid, p. 55.

39. Talking Paper (S), Lt. Col. Robert G. Morrison, Tactical Div, subj: B-57G Disposition, 29 Oct 71; hist (S/NOFORN/Gp-3), 8TFW, Oct-Dec 71, I, p. 53, and III, hist of 13 BST, p. 4.

40. Hist (S/NOFORN/Gp-3), 8TFW, Jan-Mar 72, III, hist of 13 BST.

41. Hist (S/NOFORN/Gp-3), 8TFW, Oct-Dec 71, I, p. 55.

42. Report (S/NOFORN), 7AF, subj: Commando Hunt VII, Jul 72, pp. 73, 83, 206; Background Paper (S), Lt. Col. Robert G. Morrison, Tactical Div, subj: B-57G Capability, 4 Apr 72; hist (S/NOFORN/Gp-3), 8TFW, Jan-Mar 72, III, hist of 13 BST.

Notes to pages 88 to 89

43. Hist (S/NOFORN/Gp-3), 8TFW, Jan-Mar 72, III, hist of 13 BST.

44. _Ibid_.

NOTES TO CHAPTER VI

Notes to pages 90 to 92

1. Hist (S/NOFORN/Gp-3), 8TFW, Apr-Jun 72, I, p. 22.

2. Msg (S), 8TFW to AIG 760, 111100Z Apr 72; msg (S), CINCPAC to PACAF, 092222Z Apr 72; msg (S), PACAF to CINCPAC, 190250Z Apr 72; msg (S), CINCPAC to JCS, 210252Z Apr 72; msg (S), JCS to CINCPAC, 212345Z Apr 72; msg (S), TAC to CSAF, 201606Z Apr 72.

3. Ltr (U), DAF/PRM 556p to CINCPACAF, subj: Inactivation of Pacific Air Force Units, 17 Apr 72; ltr (U), DAF/PRM 556p-1 to CINCPACAF, subj: Inactivation of Pacific Air Force Units, 12 Jun 72; ltr (U), DAF/PRM 673p to CINCPACAF, subj: Redesignation of Pacific Air Force Units, 22 Feb 73; PACAF S.O. GA-21, 1 Jul 73; ltr (U), DAF/PRM 726p to CINCPACAF, subj: Organization Actions Affecting Pacific Air Forces Units, 24 Sep 73; PACAF S.O. GA-33, 30 Sep 73.

4. Talking Paper (S), Col. Austin Joy, Asst. to Dir/Maint Eng, Dep for ANG and Reserve Affairs, subj: Status of B-57G Aircraft at 190 TR Gp (ANG), Forbes AFB, Kansas, 19 Jun 72.

5. Position Paper (S), Lt. Col. Ray T. Henderson, Tactical Div, DCS/P&O, subj: B-57G Disposition, 19 Jun 72.

6. Memo (S), Lt. Gen. George J. Eade, DCS/Plans and Operations, to Maj Gen. Donovan F. Smith, Asst DCS Plans and Operations, 22 Jun 72; memo (S), General Smith to General Eade, 23 Jun 72.

7. Memo (S), General Donovan F. Smith, Asst DCS/P&O, to Lt. Gen. George J. Eade, DCS/P&O, 23 Jun 72.

ABSTRACT

The B-57G (Tropic Moon III), 1967-1972

In March 1966, the Air Force began the Shed Light program to improve night air attack capability. Shed Light resulted in the selection of the B-57 aircraft for modification to a self-contained night attack configuration, named Tropic Moon III. More than 2 years later the Air Force awarded a contract to Westinghouse Electric Corporation to modify fifteen B-57s to the "G" configuration carrying forward looking radar, low light level television, and forward looking infrared sensors for target acquisition and identification, and a computer for weapon release.

The Tactical Air Command reactivated the 13th Bombardment Squadron, Tactical, on 8 February 1969, manned it, and more than 15 months later equipped it with B-57G aircraft. After many delays caused by equipment shortages and late aircraft delivery, the squadron flew to Ubon Royal Thai Air Force Base, Thailand, in September 1970.

One of the Tropic Moon III aircraft flew the first B-57G combat sortie over Laos on 17 October 1970, and a week later a B-57G made the first truck kill. Evaluation continued despite the failure of the primary target acquisition sensor, and the B-57G proved the practicality of the self-contained night attack aircraft under Southeast Asia conditions.

The B-57G aircraft left Thailand on 12 April 1972 for Forbes Air Force Base, Kansas, where they were flown by the Kansas Air National Guard until going into storage in early 1974.

ACRONYMS AND ABBREVIATIONS

ADTC	Armament Development and Test Center
AFAL	Air Force Armament Laboratory
AFB	Air Force Base
AFCHO	Office of the Chief of Air Force History
AFLC	Air Force Logistics Command
AFM	Air Force Manual
AFSC	Air Force Systems Command
AFSCM	Air Force Systems Command Manual
AGE	aerospace ground equipment
AGL	above ground level
ALCE	airlift control element
AMC	Air Materiel Command
ANG	Air National Guard
ANSER	Analytic Services, Inc.
APGC	Air Proving Ground Command
ASD	Aeronautical Systems Division
ATC	Air Training Command
AU	Air University
BST	Bombardment Squadron, Tactical
CCTS	Combat Crew Training Squadron
CEP	circular error probable
CINCPAC	Commander-in-Chief, Pacific
CINCPACAF	Commander-in-Chief, Pacific Air Forces
CONUS	Continental United States

CORONA HARVEST	Special project at Maxwell AFB to evaluate the effects of air operations in Southeast Asia.
CSAF	Chief of Staff, United States Air Force
DCS	Deputy Chief of Staff
DCS/P&O	Deputy Chief of Staff, Plans and Operations.
DCS/R&D	Deputy Chief of Staff, Research and Development.
DDR&E	Director of Defense, Research and Engineering
DME	distance measuring equipment
DoD	Department of Defense
ECM	electronic countermeasures
FAC	forward air controller
FLIR	forward looking infrared
FLR	forward looking radar
FOUO	for official use only
FY	fiscal year
GAO	General Accounting Office
GPO	Government Printing Office
IOC	initial operating capability
IR	infrared
JCS	Joint Chiefs of Staff
LGB	laser guided bomb
LLTV	low light level television
LOC	line(s) of communication (roads, waterways, rail lines, etc.)

LORAN	long-range aerial navigation
LTV	Ling-Temco-Vought
MAC	Military Airlift Command
Mach	The ratio of the speed of a body to the speed of sound in the surrounding atmosphere. (Mach 1 is the speed of sound; Mach 2 indicated a speed twice that of sound.)
MATS	Military Air Transport Service
MR	Memorandum
MTI	moving target indicator
OSD	Office of the Secretary of Defense
PACAF	Pacific Air Forces
P&O	Plans and Operations
PSAC	President's Scientific Advisory Council
R&D	research and development
RAF	Royal Air Force
RAM	rapid area maintenance
RFP	request for proposal
ROC	required operational capability
RTAFB	Royal Thai Air Force Base
SAF	Secretary of the Air Force
SCNA	self-contained night attack
SEA	Southeast Asia
SEAOR	Southeast Asia operational requirement
SLAR	side looking airborne radar
SO	special order

SOW	statement of work
SPO	systems project office
SWR	standing wave ratio
TAC	Tactical Air Command
TACAN	tactical air navigation
TAS	true air speed
TAWC	Tactical Air Warfare Center
TBS	Tactical Bombardment Squadron
TFA	Task Force Alpha
TFW	Tactical Fighter Wing
TI	Texas Instruments
TM-III	Tropic Moon III
TV	television
USAF	United States Air Force
VFR	visual flight rules
VR	visual reconnaissance
WRAMA	Warner-Robins Air Materiel Area

APPENDIX I -- CHRONOLOGY

<u>7 February 1966</u> (S) Gen. James Ferguson, Deputy Chief of Staff for Research and Development, HQ USAF, established a task force, Shed Light, within his staff to ". . . clarify the capability as well as the limitations of the night attack problem. . . ."

<u>February 1966</u> (S) The Air Force assigned the 433d and 479th Tactical Fighter Squadrons of the 8th Tactical Fighter Wing, Ubon Royal Thai Air Force Base, the sole mission of night interdiction.

<u>5 March 1966</u> (U) The Shed Light Task Force, whose mission was to improve night air combat operations, concluded its Phase I study, listing 29 proposals to improve night navigation, target acquisition, and ordnance delivery.

<u>18 March 1966</u> (U) An Air Force-wide Shed Light program began, with the objective of achieving a creditable tactical night attack capability in the shortest practicable time.

<u>9 June 1967</u> (S) The Aeronautical Systems Division submitted to the Air Staff a proposal that envisioned nearly simultaneous research, development, aircraft modification, equipment testing, and personnel training.

<u>28 September 1967</u> (U) The General Officers' Shed Light review meeting decided to modify the B-57 to a self-contained night attack configuration named Tropic Moon III.

<u>7 October 1967</u> (S) The Tactical Air Command issued Required Operational Capability 62-67 calling for a night attack wing composed of three B-57 squadrons and a composite Shed Light squadron of NC-123, RC-130, S2D, and A-1E aircraft.

October 1967 (S) The Air Staff directed implementation of Tropic Moon III, the conversion of B-57s to self-contained night attack aircraft.

12 February 1968 (U) Secretary of the Air Force Harold Brown asked the Secretary of Defense for approval to reprogram $52 million for Tropic Moon III.

8 March 1968 (S) The Aerospace Systems Division released a Request for Proposal and Statement of Work to 20 prospective contractors.

May 1968 (C) Air Force headquarters issued an aircraft modification requirement to initiate the third phase of the Tropic Moon program--the "G" configuration of the B-57 Canberra jet bomber. Phase I had involved installation of low light level television in A-1E aircraft for testing in Southeast Asia, and Phase II had called for installation of improved low light level television in three B-57s.

15 July 1968 (U) The Air Force awarded a contract to Westinghouse Electric Corporation, Baltimore, Md, for the "G" configuration systems to be installed in a small number of B-57 aircraft.

August 1968 (S) Martin began refurbishing two B-57Bs, the first of 15 to be modified by Westinghouse.

8 February 1969 (U) The Tactical Air Command reactivated the 13th Bombardment Squadron, Tactical, and assigned it to the 15th Tactical Fighter Wing, MacDill Air Force Base, Florida.

30 June 1969 (C) Air Force investment in the B-57G initial spares program reached a total of $23.4 million obligated.

18 July 1969 (S) Westinghouse began Category I testing of B-57Gs.

28 October 1969 (S) The Air Force accepted the first B-57G and began Category II testing.

30 November 1969 (C) The original TM-III/B-57G program schedule called for delivery of all B-57G aircraft to MacDill Air Force Base by this date. None had been delivered.

16 December 1969 (U) A B-57G crashed during a Category I test flight near Baltimore, MD.

12 February 1970 (U) Maj. Gen. A.J. Beck, Warner Robins Air Materiel Area commander and a number of his staff officers visited Texas Instruments on logistical support matters related to the gunship programs and to the forthcoming B-57G deployment.

March 1970 (C) The original program schedule called for completion of all B-57G crew training during this month so that the aircraft could be sent to Southeast Asia prior to the end of the month. The goal was not met.

11 March 1970 (S) Air Force headquarters announced that the B-57G would be sent to Southeast Asia in September 1970.

29 April 1970 (U) Category III testing of the B-57G began.

22 May 1970 (U) The 13th Bombardment Squadron, Tactical, received its first B-57G aircraft.

29 May 1970 (C) The first operational training flight of the newly configured B-57G aircraft was conducted at MacDill Air Force Base.

15 June 1970 (C) By this date, B-57G spares program obligations had reached $26.7 million.

June 1970 (S) Westinghouse announced a cost overrun of $4.95 million and warned that the amount could go much higher.

16 July 1970 (U) The Tactical Air Command commander recommended delaying the deployment of the B-57G.

4 August 1970 (C) B-57G aircraft scheduled for operational use in Southeast Asia in September 1970 began arriving at MacDill AFB for crew training purposes.

31 August 1970 (U) Project Code 253 was assigned to B-57G spares and repairables being delivered to and from the repair contractor.

August 1970 (C) Revised TM-III/B-57G program schedule called for delivery of all B-57G aircraft to MacDill AFB during this month. The schedule change resulted from problems encountered in subsystem design and incorporation of changes required as a result of Category I and II testing.

August-September 1970 (C) B-57G deployment plans drawn up following the General Officers' Board's recommendation called for the return of the aircraft to the factory for removal of sensors prior to take-off for the flight to Southeast Asia. The equipment would be reinstalled at the Royal Thai Air Force Base Ubon, Thailand.

5 September 1970 (U) The Air Force Chief of Staff directed deployment on 15 September.

28 September 1970 (C) The first B-57G aircraft arrived at Ubon Thailand.

30 September 1970 (C) Transfer of eleven B-57G aircraft of the 13th Bombardment Squadron, Tactical from MacDill AFB to the Royal Thai AFB, Ubon, Thailand, was completed.

10 October 1970 (U) The Commando Hunt V interdiction campaign in Laos began.

17 October 1970 (U) The 13th Bombardment Squadron flew the first B-57G combat sortie over Laos.

24 October 1970 (U) The 13th Bombardment Squadron recorded the first truck kill by a B-57G.

3 December 1970 (S) An in-flight fire severaly damaged the wing of a B-57G aircraft. It was out of commission for more than 2 months while a replacement wing was flown to Ubon, modified and mounted.

12 December 1970 (C) The first B-57G combat loss took place. This reduced the number of operational B-57Gs in SEA to nine.

14 December 1970 (U) Daily newspapers throughout the country carried the first-known reports of B-57G operations in Southeast Asia, with the announcement of the first loss of a B-57G to enemy action in Laos. The "G" configuration of the B-57 Canberra bomber was a highly classified project.

13 January 1971 (U) Air Force Systems Command headquarters hosted a meeting to discuss and coordinate a test program to identify the problems and evaluate the fixes for the APQ-139 forward-looking radar in the B-57G aircraft.

11 February 1971 (C) The Warner Robins Air Materiel Area Rapid Area Maintenance team completed replacing the B-57G wing.

15 February 1971 (U) A story in U.S. News and World Report about the operations of the B-57G and the AC-119 and AC-130 gunships in Southeast Asia also mentioned the sensors carried by those aircraft.

1 May 1971 (U) Commando Hunt V ended.

July 1971 (S) The Seventh Air Force decided the B-57Gs would fly normal daytime bombing missions over Cambodia.

4 August 1971 (S) Gen. John D. Ryan, Air Force Chief of Staff, asked the Joint Chiefs of Staff to authorize the return of the 13th Bombardment Squadron to the United States to make room in Thailand for other units.

4 September 1971 (S) Secretary of Defense Melvin R. Laird approved a waiver of the Thailand manpower ceiling to allow the 13th Bombardment Squadron to remain in Thailand until January 1972.

1 November 1971 (U) Commando Hunt VII, the interdiction campaign over Laos, began.

9 November 1971 (S) Modified APQ-139 radars had been installed in all B-57Gs at Ubon Royal Thai Air Force Base.

10 November 1971 (S) The Seventh Air Force discontinued daytime bombing missions by B-57G aircraft over Cambodia.

November 1971 (S) Pacific Air Forces alerted the 13th Bombardment Squadron to be ready to return to the United States in May.

23 December 1971 (S) Secretary of Defense Laird agreed to retain the 13th at Ubon through the dry season in Laos.

February 1972 (S) Pacific Air Forces again alerted the 13th to be ready to return to the United States in May.

12 April 1972 (U) The B-57G aircraft left Ubon.

20 April 1972 (S) The Tactical Command cancelled Required Operational Commitment 62-67 which 4 years earlier had generated the original Tropic Moon III actions.

23 June 1972 (S) Gen. Horace M. Wade, Vice Chief of Staff of the Air Force, decided that the B-57Gs would remain in the Air National Guard rather than being stored.

June 1972 (U) All B-57Gs arrived at Forbes AFB, Kansas.

24 December 1972 (S) Pacific Air Forces transferred the 13th Bombardment Squadron to Clark Air Base without personnel or equipment and assigned it to the 405th Fighter Wing.

1 July 1973 (S) The Air Force redesignated the 13th Bombardment Squadron the 13th Fighter Squadron.

30 September 1973 (S) Pacific Air Forces redesignated the 13th Fighter Squadron the 13th Bombardment Squadron, Tactical, and inactivated it.

APPENDIX II -- KEY PERSONNEL

(U) Because of the large number of names and throughout this study, a listing of those names should be helpful to the reader. Ranks or titles and positions listed with each name are those held at the time the individual was connected with the B-57G program.

BECK, A.J., Major General, Commander, WRAMA.

BLANCHARD, William H., General, Vice Chief of Staff, Headquarters, U.S. Air Force.

BOLENDER, Carroll H., Brigadier General, Deputy Director of Development and Acquisition, Headquarters, U.S. Air Force.

BOYLAN, George S., Lieutenant General, DCS/Programs and Resources, Headquarters, U.S. Air Force.

BROWN, Harold, Dr., Director, Defense Research and Engineering; Secretary of the Air Force

BURNS, Kenneth P., Major, staff officer assigned to the Directorate of Plans and Operations, Headquarters, U.S. Air Force.

BUSCHETTE, Edwin A., Lieutenant Colonel, Senior Sensor Operator, 13th BST.

CLARK, John A., Lieutenant Colonel, pilot, 13th BST.

CLAY, Lucius D., General, Commander, Seventh Air Force, CINCPACAF.

CODY, Joseph J., Jr., Major General, Chief of Staff, AFSC.

CORRIE, Worth H., Colonel, Assistant to the Director of Development for Shed Light.

EADE, George J., Lieutenant General, DCS/Plans and Operations, Headquarters, U.S. Air Force.

EVANS, Andrew J., Major General, Director of Development, Headquarters, U.S. Air Force; Commander, Tactical Air Warfare Center.

FERGUSON, James, Lieutenant General, Deputy Chief of Staff for R&D, Headquarters, U.S. Air Force; Commander, Air Force Systems Command.

FLAX, Alexander H., Dr., Assistant Secretary of the Air Force for R&D.

FOSTER, John S., Dr., Director, Defense Research and Engineering.

GARWIN, Richard L., Dr., Member, President's Scientific Advisory Council.

HARGROVE, Clifford W., Major General, Deputy Director of Operations, Headquarters, U.S. Air Force.

HARRIS, Hunter, J., General, CINCPACAF

HOLZAPPLE, Joseph R., Lieutenant General, DCS/R&D, Headquarters, U.S. Air Force.

HORNIG, Donald F., Dr., Science Advisor to President Johnson..

JOHNSON, Lyndon B., President of the United States.

KOSAN, Douglas J., Major, B-57G Sensor Operator, 13th BST.

KUCHEMEN, Henry B., Jr., Major General, Commander, Aeronautical Systems Division.

LAIRD, Melvin R., Secretary of Defense.

MATTHEWS, Edward K., Lieutenant Colonel, Commander, 13th BST, 1971-72.

McCAIN, John S., Jr., Admiral, USN, CINCPAC, 1972.

McCONNELL, John P., General, Chief of Staff, U.S. Air Force.

McNAMARA, Robert S., Secretary of Defense.

McRAE Vincent V., Dr., Staff Member, Office of Science Adviser to President Johnson.

MERRELL, Jack G., General, Commander AFLC.

MEYER, John C., General, Vice Chief of Staff, Headquarters, U.S. Air Force.

MEYERS, Gilbert C., Major General, Deputy Commander, 2d Air Div.

MOMYER, William W., General, Commander, Seventh Air Force; Commander, Tactical Air Command.

MOORE, William G., Major General, Director of Operational Requirements and Development Plans, DCS/R&D, Headquarters, U.S. Air Force.

NITZE, Paul H., Deputy Secretary of Defense.

O'NEILL, John W., Lieutenant General, Vice Commander, Air Force Systems Command.

PITT, Paul R., Lieutenant Colonel, Commander, 13th BST.

ROTHLISBERGER, William O., Major, Pilot, 13th BST.

RYAN, John D., General, CINCPACAF; Air Force Chief of Staff.

SCHINZ, Albert W., Major General, Commander, Tactical Air Warfare Center; DCS/Operations, Headquarters, Tactical Air Command.

SCHRIEVER, Bernard A., General, Commander, Air Force Systems Command.

SEAMANS, Robert C., Secretary of the Air Force.

SIHANOUK, NORODOM, Prince, Cambodian ruler, later deposed.

SILVIA, Ronald, Captain, Sensor Operator, 13th BST.

SMITH, Donovan, F., Major General, Assistant DCS/P&O, Headquarters, U.S. Air Force.

SMITH, William Y., Colonel, Military Assistant to the Secretary of the Air Force.

VANCE, Cyrus R., Deputy Secretary of Defense.

VOGT, John W., Major General, DCS/P&O, PACAF.

DISTRIBUTION

1.	SAFOS		55.	AFISC/HO
2.	SAFUS		56-57.	AFLC/HO
3.	SAFAL		58.	AFMPC/DPMEOI
4.	SAFMI		59.	AFOSI/HO
5.	SAFFM		60-61.	AFRES/HO
6.	SAFIA		62-68.	AFSC/HO
7.	SAFGC		69.	AFTAC/HO
8.	SAFLL		70.	ARPC/HO
9.	SAFOI		71-72.	ATC/HO
10.	SAFAA		73.	AU/HO
11.	SAFAAR		74.	AFMEA/OI
			75-76.	MAC/CSH
12.	AFCC		77-78.	PACAF/HO
13.	AFCV		79-80.	SAC/HO
14.	AFCVA		81-84.	TAC/HO
15.	AFCCN		85.	USAFA/HO
			86-87.	USAFE/HO
16.	AFCVS		88.	AFTEC/HO
			89.	USAFSS/HO
17.	AFIG		90.	AULD

18. AFJA

OTHER

19. AFIN

91-92. AFSHRC
93-115. AF/CVAH(S)(Stock)

20-26. AFPA (For Internal Distribution)

27-35. AFXO (For Internal Distribution)

36-41. AFRD (For Internal Distribution)

42-46. AFLE (For Internal Distribution)

47. NGB

MAJOR COMMANDS

48. AAC/HO
49. ADCOM/HO
50. AFAA/CE
51. AFAFC/HO
52. AFCS/HO
53. AFDAA/HO
54. AFIS/HO

www.ingramcontent.com/pod-product-compliance
Lightning Source LLC
Chambersburg PA
CBHW081617170426
43195CB00041B/2860